Caldecott Connections to Science

Caldecott Connections to Science

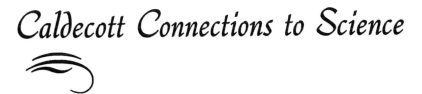

Shan Glandon

2000
LIBRARIES UNLIMITED
A Member of Greenwood Publishing, Inc.
Westport, Connecticut • London

To the investigator and problem solver in each of us . . . celebrate curiosity and questioning.

Libraries Unlimited
A member of Greenwood Publishing Group, Inc.
88 Post Road West,
Westport, CT 06881
www.lu.com

Library of Congress Cataloging-in-Publication Data

Glandon, Shan.
Caldecott connections to science / Shan Glandon.
p. cm.
Includes bibliographical references and index.
ISBN 1-56308-687-5 (paper)
1. Science--Study and teaching (Elementary)--United States--Curricula. 2. Caldecott Medal. 3. Illustrated children's books--Study and teaching--United States. 4. Education, Elementary--Activity programs--United States. I. Title.

LB1585.3 .G53 2000
372.3'5044-dc21

00-027967

10 9 8 7 6 5

Contents

10—*A Tree Is Nice* (*continued*)

11—*The Caldecott Award*

Figures and Activity Sheets

Figures

Activity Sheets

Introduction

➤ Connecting to the Curriculum

Caldecott Award literature provides rich fuel for teaching, extending, and enriching curriculum objectives. The award winners are engaging stories that offer vivid vocabulary images, use art in varied ways, and spark links to each of the major curriculum areas.

Students may begin the year with a look at Randolph Caldecott and the award itself (see the lesson on introducing Randolph Caldecott and reading the honor books on p. 221), and Caldecott Award posters may be displayed in the classroom and the library as a constant visual reminder of the stories that have won. (Caldecott Award posters are available for $2.00 from Perma-Bound, 617 East Vandalia Rd., Jacksonville, IL 62650, 800-637-6581.) The Caldecott Medal, named in honor of Randolph Caldecott, a nineteenth-century children's book illustrator, has been awarded annually since 1938 to an American illustrator for the most distinguished picture book published during the previous year. When reviewing books for the award, committee members look for excellence in artistic technique and in integrating the text of the story into the pictorial interpretation. Randolph Caldecott was chosen because he established new directions in children's book illustration; he drew with the child in mind. His illustrations combine humor and imagination and are filled with lifelike characters, a lot of action, and many details. Bookmark the Caldecott Web site, <http://www.ala.org/alsc/caldecott.html>, and students can browse for further information and enjoyment (accessed February 2000).

➤ Connecting to Art

Connections with art teachers are a natural result of focusing on Caldecott Award literature and offer opportunities for students to try different illustration techniques as they explore line, color, tone, and balance in art. After reading and experiencing *A Tree Is Nice*, students can create their own imaginative watercolor washed with gouache scenes of favorite tree memories. For a dramatization of *Frog Went A-Courtin'*, the students can construct delightful animal masks and headdresses representing the main characters and the guests at the wedding, using large brown paper bags, black markers for outlining and details, and tempera paints for filling in lines with bright colors. In creating *The Snowy Day* collages, students can discover the effectiveness of placing real objects and found materials in their scenes. Watercolor paintings (like those in *Sylvester and the Magic Pebble*) provide students with opportunities to play with color to express mood and emotion in art, while colored pencil doodles give students fun with scribbles that can emerge into shapes and scenes like those found in *Song and Dance Man*. Woodcut illustrations (*A Story, a Story*) can be created using foam trays, scratching tools, and different colors of ink.

Another method for helping students experience the variety of media used in illustrating Caldecott Award literature is to gather samples of the different media. Take a trip to an art supply store and purchase the following supplies: paint samples (oil, acrylic, watercolor, gouache, gesso, and tempera), paintbrushes, a pen with a number of nibs, inks (India and one other), pastels (oil, Conté, and one other), pencils (grease, graphite, and colored), a small block of soft wood like pine or balsa (for woodcuts), and an Exacto knife (for the woodcuts). As the stories are shared and the art techniques are discussed, show the appropriate media and demonstrate their uses.

➤ Connecting to Units

Caldecott Award stories can become the springboard for introducing units of studies. The science connections increase students' abilities to observe and classify, hypothesize, experiment, draw conclusions, and communicate results. Earth science topics focus on geology and changes in the Earth's crust (*The Funny Little Woman*), the moon (*Many Moons*), and the weather (*Sylvester and the Magic Pebble*). Life science inquiries concentrate on habitats (*Make Way for Ducklings*), interdependence (*Frog Went A-Courtin'*), the human body (*Song and Dance Man*), spiders and insects (*A Story, a Story*), trees (*A Tree Is Nice*), and zoo animals (*One Fine Day*). Physical science investigations allow students to examine the world of matter (*The Snowy Day*).

➤ Collaboration

Collaboration between classroom teachers and library media specialists facilitates implementation of the activities described in this book. The stories can be shared in the classroom or the library, and both the teacher and the librarian can assign, develop, and assess activities. The duck unit (using *Make Way for Ducklings*) requires this close connection because students use the multiple resources of the library to work as scientists, writers, and performers. In the weather unit, which develops from *Sylvester and the Magic Pebble*, the library media specialist and the teacher can divide mentoring responsibilities and help students effectively work through the steps of the writing process by creating weather riddles, poems, and folk stories. Research is also a significant component of this unit as students work in teams to find out about clouds, fog, and dew. Multiple resources (on caves, canyons, earthquakes, and volcanoes) can be provided by the library media specialist for the geology unit, which evolves from sharing *The Funny Little Woman*. Discovery centers offer independent exploration experiences and more in-depth studies, and the library can be a vital link in making these happen; several of the stories provide these learning opportunities (*The Funny Little Woman, Make Way for Ducklings*, and *Many Moons*). The library media specialist may give book talks to help students select animal nonfiction choices for independent reading and for researching ways in which animals adapt (*One Fine Day*). The space and resources of the library are more conducive to doing frog and pond life research and offer a large area in which to create the pond life mural (*Frog Went A-Courtin'*), as well as provide research time for investigating spiders and insects (*A Story, a Story*).

When implementing the *Many Moons* lesson plans, the following pattern of collaboration between the classroom and the library occurred. The story was introduced by the librarian; during the creative problem-solving exercise, both the teacher and the librarian circulated and facilitated the process. The librarian led the Facts About the Moon research lesson, and at the "Connect" stage of the lesson plan, the teacher showed the discovery center task cards and introduced the activities. Then the students returned to the classroom to select their investigations and complete preliminary planning. (This particular teacher used centers as a way of organizing the class during his two literature circle times. While he worked with one small group, the rest of the students rotated through the centers.) During literature circle/center time, four activities took place: the literature circle meeting with the teacher and the three discovery centers (set up in the classroom). While the teacher met with the first literature circle (usually for an hour), the rest of the students were divided among the discovery center activities. The students working in "A Shadow on the Moon" and "Changes in the Moon" discovery centers returned to the library in search of research information on eclipses and phases of the moon. The librarian also mentored students as they developed their demonstrations and skits. Some students who chose the "Traveling to the Moon" investigation returned to the library to check out space flight books, and others met together in the classroom to begin brainstorming ideas for their letters. This pattern of work was repeated while the teacher met with the second literature circle. Discovery center investigations were assessed by the librarian and recorded as a science grade in the classroom. The gravity, satellite, and surface of the moon lessons were completed in the library, and the entire class (with their teacher) came every day for a week for an hour of work time. Lunar rovers were demonstrated and displayed in the media center. For the culminating Lunar Disaster activity, the class met in the library so that students could spread out during small group time.

The lessons resulting from sharing *Song and Dance Man* followed this pattern of collaboration: The story was introduced in the library, and in the classroom the teacher followed the story with The Human Body Machine lesson plan. (Students created a mind map of ideas and a bulletin board display showing the workings of the human body.) The next lesson plan, Energy for the Body—The Ingredients, required two research sessions in the library, but students developed their products (the human body drawing, the model, and the report) in the classroom. The lesson plan Energy for the Body—Delivery occurred in the classroom; during the discovery center phase of the Protecting the Body—Skin and Hair and Nails, some students worked in the library and some students worked in the classroom. The lessons Protecting the Body—Bones; Control—Messages to and from the Brain; Coordination—The Muscles of the Body; and Generations all occurred under the direction of the teacher in the classroom. For the culminating vaudeville show, students rehearsed and presented in the library.

The library truly becomes an extension of the classroom and provides key ingredients for the successful implementation of the lesson plans.

➤ Integrating Multiple Intelligences Theory and Practice

In *Frames of Mind: The Theory of Multiple Intelligences* (New York: Basic Books, 1983), Howard Gardner challenges the narrowly held definition of intelligence (based on an IQ score) and the context in which IQ had been measured (completing isolated tasks outside of a natural learning environment) and proposes a theory of multiple intelligences that identifies at least eight basic intelligences and defines intelligence as the capacity for solving problems and fashioning products in a context-rich and naturalistic setting. *Verbal/linguistic intelligence* is the capacity to use words effectively, either in writing (exemplified by poets, authors, playwrights, journalists, and editors) or in speaking (storytelling and debating). Students who evidence this intelligence pore over words, are fascinated with language, and use language effectively in speaking and/or in writing. Those with *musical/rhythmic intelligence* respond to sounds and rhythms and enjoy and seek out opportunities to hear music, to improvise and play with sounds and rhythms, and to mentor with musicians. Notice these students: They often tap their feet or pencils, sometimes hum while working intently, and perk up when music or rhythm is used during a lesson. *Visual/spatial intelligence* is defined by an ability to see the visual/spatial world accurately and to act upon those images through painting, drawing, designing, and sculpting. Because they see internally, students with highly developed visual/spatial intelligence are often good at chess and navigation (finding their way in uncharted spaces); they may also be day-dreamers. These are the artists who love anything visual, who see images and pictures and draw their ideas. *Bodily/kinesthetic intelligence* is found in dancers, athletes, and inventors because of their prowess in using body movement to express ideas and feelings and to implement game plays or use their hands to create new products or transform things. Think of students who learn best by doing; if they can manipulate it, do it, create movements to learn it, then they develop understanding. *Logical/mathematical intelligence* involves skill with numbers and number manipulation and skill in strategies for reasoning— scientific, deductive, and inductive. Problem solving interests these students, and they love the challenge of organizing and using numbers and developing charts, timelines, and graphs as expressions of thinking. Students with highly developed *interpersonal intelligence* easily communicate and work collaboratively with others; they are sensitive to feelings and moods. These students are good listeners who work well in collaborative situations and seem to get along with anyone. They have a knack for bringing out the best in each learner. *Intrapersonal intelligence* focuses on self-knowledge and the ability to act on the basis of that knowledge. These students are reflective, thoughtful learners who need to see the big picture and have time to fit new knowledge into current thinking; they enjoy building awareness of their own processes for learning. The eighth intelligence, the *naturalist intelligence*, describes a student's ability to observe, see patterns, and make connections in living things (plants and animals) and in natural phenomena (clouds, rocks). This intelligence highlights the accomplishments of scientists in creating classification systems.

Gardner suggests that everyone possesses all eight intelligences, but some are highly developed, others more modestly developed, and still others relatively undeveloped, and that most people can develop each intelligence to an adequate level of competency. This understanding has implications for the organization and development of daily lesson plans because integration of multiple intelligences theory and practice expands opportunities for students to mobilize their full range of intellectual abilities and become thoroughly engaged in learning.

➤ Designing the Lessons

Best-practice principles emerging from state-of-the-art teaching in each curriculum field focus on learning that is student-centered (builds on students' natural curiosity), experiential (is hands-on and active), holistic (involves big-picture ideas), authentic (involves encounters with complex and real ideas), expressive (demands the whole range of intelligence, art, music, writing, speaking, etc.), reflective (allows time to generalize and make connections), social (includes support of peers and mentors), collaborative (encourages working together rather than in competition), democratic (models the principles of living and working in a democracy), cognitive (demands higher-order thinking), developmental (involves learning experiences guided by the needs of the students), constructivist (builds, creates, and develops knowledge systems), and challenging (provides choices and responsibility for learning). Two books to read for more information about these principles are *Best Practices* by Steven Zemelman, Harvey Daniels, and Arthur Hyde (Heinemann, 1998), and *ITI: The Model, Integrated Thematic Instruction* by Susan Kovalik (Books for Educators, 1994). They can be ordered from Heinemann, 361 Hanover St., Portsmouth, NH 03801-3912; cost: $23.50, and Books for Educators, 17051 S.E. 272d St., Suite 18, Kent, WA, 98042; cost: $27.50.

The "Engage, Elaborate, Explore, Connect" lesson plan format that I developed in 1994 is the organizing structure for the story units in this book. This lesson planning format integrates best-practice principles, builds a discovery approach to learning, promotes integration of multiple intelligences theory and practice, and lets teachers see, at a glance, diversity and flexibility in teaching.

Engage

Teachers use this one- to-three-minute step to engage the attention of the student; it's a wake-up call to the brain—a way to start the brain thinking about patterns and relationships. Through a puzzling picture, a catchy musical piece, a challenging question, complicated body movements, a paradox, or a series of quick visual images, the "Engage" step provides the spark that captures the interest of the students and prepares them for the lesson content.

Elaborate

In this portion of the lesson, teachers use multiple intelligence strategies to elaborate important concepts and skills. Teachers may use stories, video footage, creative dramatics, debate, dance and movement, questioning, and rhythms to teach lesson content.

Explore

This step gives the students opportunities to explore lesson content and develop in-depth investigations and studies.

Connect

This is the step in which students make connections to real-world settings through reflection, generalization, synthesis, and transformation, thus enhancing the capacity for solving problems and fashioning products.

When using this organizing format, there are many starting points. Sometimes the "Explore" activity is clear in my mind and I work from that activity. I then decide what direct instruction is needed for successful completion of the activity. (This direct instruction becomes the "Elaborate" stage of the lesson.) With these two components developed, I think about capturing students' attention, awakening the brain for learning, and sparking an interest. The "Engage" step of the lesson helps students tune in and get ready for the complexity of thought and work required for the rest of the lesson. Music, art, and movement are particularly effective attention-getters in the "Engage" step, and I enjoy challenging myself to use them. Based on these three components of the lesson, I think about making connections and demonstrating understandings and ask myself this question: How will students reflect on the activity and demonstrate and share what they have learned?

For science lessons, the "Connect" understanding is my starting point (e.g., an animal's survival depends on its ability to adapt), and I imagine and think of lessons that will contribute to this understanding and offer opportunities to work and think as scientists in real-world settings do. In trying to get the students to work and think as scientists, I am guided by these inquiry processes: observation, classification, questioning, experimentation, interpretation, and communication. Lessons with these processes integrated into them result in active, hands-on learning experiences that demand multiple intelligences and encounters with real-world settings.

Caldecott Connections to Science brings award-winning literature to all areas of the science curriculum. I hope you enjoy the fun and diversity offered in the activities and the noise and excitement produced when students are actively engaged in constructing knowledge. I also hope these activities inspire continuing connections for you and your students.

1 Frog Went A-Courtin'

Retold by John Langstaff
Illustrated by Feodor Rojankovsky
New York: Harcourt, Brace, 1955

Summary

➤ Frog went calling on Mistress Mouse and asked her to marry him. Uncle Rat gave his consent and the wedding plans were started: The place is way down yonder in the hollow tree, the breakfast will be three green beans and a black-eyed pea, and the wedding dress will be made by Old Miss Rat from Pumpkin Town. They celebrate the wedding with their small animal and insect friends until the arrival of the old tom cat, when they are all forced to scatter for safety.

Award Year

➤ 1956

Art Information

➤ Illustrated using brush, ink, and crayon; alternates between four-color illustrations and two-color illustrations (black and green).

Curriculum Connections

➤ Frogs, with emphasis on this science idea: Frogs are part of the pond community; their survival and the survival of the pond as a whole depends on the interrelationships of the organisms that live there.

➤ Activity Plan 1: Sharing the Story

Materials

Chart paper
Marker
Green and black crayons
Caldecott Award poster
Pen and ink
Crayons (black, green, red, yellow)

Engage

Have students pretend to be frogs and act out the poem in figure 1.1. (*Bodily/Kinesthetic Intelligence*)

Little green frogs by a stream are we.
(Crouch like frogs.)

Hoppity, hop, hop, jump, jump, jump!
(Begin to jump like frogs.)

We sun on lily pads, smooth and dry,
(Pretend to settle on a lily pad.)

And watch birds and insects as they fly by.
(Move eyes from left to right and up and down,
pretending to search for insects.)

Then, splash! How we make the water fly!
(Jump into the water and clap your hands as you
jump.)

Hoppity, hop, hop, jump, jump, jump!
(Jump like frogs.)

➤ Figure 1.1. Frog Poem

Elaborate

Introduce the story and ask students to look for patterns in the story (both in the words and in the illustrations) as you read.

Explore

Discuss the language patterns in this story (the story is written in couplets and has a singsong rhythm) and identify the rhyming lines. Have students brainstorm ideas for new guests to ask to the wedding. Whom might they invite? What might these new guests bring to the wedding or wedding reception? Create a chart listing the guests and the gifts they bring. Following are some examples:

Guest	Gift
rat	new hat
black widow spider	jug of cider
brown bear	juicy pear
grasshopper	bracelets of copper
earthworm	influenza germ
goat	sailboat
Garibaldi the fish	dish
whale	pail
dog	fog

Connect

Share the Caldecott Award information:

1. As students examine the cover of the book, ask them if there is anything special that they notice. (gold medal) Ask them to name the medal. (Caldecott Award Medal) Ask them if they know why it has been placed on this book. (Expect some of the following answers: The illustrations are special, well done, particularly interesting, exciting, and/or unusual.)

2. Discuss the art techniques used in creating the pictures. Browse the illustrations once again and identify the contrasts: a pattern of two pages in full color followed by two pages in black and green. Spend time on the full-color illustrations showing the arrival of Uncle Rat, because these really show the combination of crayon (Uncle Rat's robe, the door, the spinning wheel, the staircase) and ink (the fur of both animals).

3. Ask two student volunteers to search the Caldecott Award poster for the year in which the story won. (Searching the poster helps students become familiar with the many different titles selected for the award.)

Review how to write a couplet. Have the students use the words in the list to create their own couplets. The words that end each line must rhyme (repeat some examples from the book). Each line should have the same number of syllables (use some lines from the book and count the syllables). *Note:* If couplet writing is too difficult, have students brainstorm the new guest list and the gifts or contributions they bring. Then write the couplets yourself and present them to the students for illustrating.

Following are some couplets that students wrote using the words from the list above:

> With the arrival of the fat brown rat,
> Miss Mousie had a wonderful new hat.
>
> Then came the black widow spider,
> She brought extra jugs of cider.
>
> Next to come in was a great brown bear,
> She brought a chair and a tasty pear.
>
> Next to come in was Mister Grasshopper,
> He brought shiny bracelets made from copper.
>
> Next to come in was Charlie the earthworm,
> Achoo! He had the influenza germ.
>
> Next to come in was the old billy goat,
> Smoothly sailing in his bright red sailboat.
>
> Next to come in was Garibaldi the fish,
> He served chocolate chip ice cream from a dish.
>
> Next to come in was the blue whale,
> He brought tasty fish in a pail.
>
> Next to come in was Spotty the dog,
> His arrival brought thick "pea soup" fog.

Have students work with partners and write new rhyming couplets for the story. Illustrate the rhymes, but only use green and black, like the illustrations in the book. Gather the pages into a new book. (*Interpersonal, Verbal/Linguistic, and Visual/Spatial Intelligences*)

➤ Activity Plan 2: The Life of a Frog

Materials

Drawing paper
Illustrating materials (markers, crayons, colored pencils, chalk)
Old nature magazines

Nonfiction book about frogs (*Frogs* by Gail Gibbons [New York: Holiday House, 1993] is a good choice; it has simple but factual text and great illustrations.)

Frog eggs (Available from Carolina Biological Supply Company, P.O. Box 6010, Burlington, NC 27215, 800-334-5551; cost: $19.50 for 100–150 eggs.)

Aquarium (Ask for a donation from parents, browse garage sales, or purchase an inexpensive one from a store.)

Science journals

Engage

The class's first look at frogs began on the imaginary side—the wedding of Mistress Mouse and Frog. Now begin looking at the facts with a dramatization of the life cycle of a frog.

To assess prior knowledge, ask students to identify the stages in the life of a frog; probable answers will be *egg, tadpole, frog*. Have students dramatize the stages using the following movements. (*Bodily/Kinesthetic Intelligence*)

Frog Life Cycle Dramatization

1. Egg: Lie on your side and curl into a tight ball.

2. Tadpole: Turn on your stomach and try to move like a tadpole.

3. Young frog: Crouch and hop like a frog.

Elaborate

Share the nonfiction book about frogs and ask students to listen carefully for more information about the life cycle of frogs. Discuss what they have learned and brainstorm an expanded list of the life stages of frogs.

Explore

Have students draw their understanding using a circle flow chart (see figure 1.2). Have them cut pictures from magazines, print out clip art from the computer, or create original art to illustrate the flow chart. Have students share their drawings. (*Visual/Spatial Intelligence*)

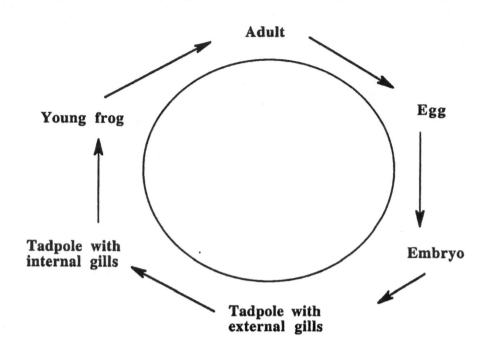

Adult

Young frog

Egg

**Tadpole with
internal gills**

Embryo

**Tadpole with
external gills**

➤Figure 1.2. Frog's Life Cycle

Connect

Introduce the aquarium and the frog eggs. Set up a schedule for observing the aquarium and encourage students to use their science journals to record daily observations and changes. As a fun closing, have students dramatize again the life cycle of the frog adding the new stages they have learned.

Frog Life Cycle Dramatization

1. Egg: Lie on your side and curl into a tight ball.

2. Embryo: Slowly begin to stretch out but stay on your side, and keep your feet and legs together.

3. Tadpole with external gills: Turn on your stomach. Try to move like a tadpole using your hands as feathery outside gills. Breathe deeply in and out.

4. Tadpole with internal gills: Do same movement, except breathe more shallowly, opening and closing your mouth like a fish.

5. Young frog: Crouch and make small jumps.

➤ Activity Plan 3: Avoiding Danger—Predators

Materials

Outdoor setting (Look for a space that has places to hide, such as trees, bushes, or dips in the terrain.)

Book on animal camouflage (*Animal Camouflage* by Joyce Powzyk [New York: Bradbury Press, 1990] has a lot of pictures of hard-to-find animals.)

Drawing paper

Illustrating materials (markers, crayons, colored pencils, chalk)

Scissors

Guide book showing different kinds of frogs (*National Audubon Society, First Field Guide: Amphibians* by Brian Cassie [New York: Scholastic, 1999] is a good one.)

Engage

Walk to the outdoor setting and play the predator/prey game. One student is the predator searching for prey. The predator must close his or her eyes until prey are camouflaged. Then the predator may stoop, stand on tiptoes, and pivot to find the prey. The predator cannot move from the selected spot. The rest of the students are prey and must hide from the predator; however, the prey must be able to see the predator at all times because it's important to watch the moves of the predator. The prey must keep the predator in sight at all times, and the predator must carefully examine the landscape in all directions in order to locate prey. Play the game several times. You will notice that students become more adept at camouflage and hiding as they play. Choose a new predator each time you play. (*Bodily/Kinesthetic Intelligence*)

Elaborate

Discuss what happened during the game. How did students hide themselves? How did they adapt themselves to the hiding places available in the outdoor setting?

Make a three-column list on the board, labeling the columns as *Eggs/embryos*, *Tadpoles*, and *Frogs*. Have students research and list predators of the frog for each stage of life. (Figure 1.3 lists many of the predators.)

1. As students analyze the chart, ask them which stages they think are the most dangerous in terms of predators. Why? (The egg/embryo and tadpole stages are most dangerous because the frog doesn't have as many protection strategies.)

2. Ask the students how a frog might protect itself from enemies. Answers you might hear include a frog's ability to escape by jumping, by plunging into the water in search of a hiding place, or by swimming quickly away from the predator. Frogs also have keen eyesight and sharp hearing, which help them detect danger; it's hard to surprise a frog. Another structure is a frog's ability to puff: Frogs swallow air and puff themselves up to appear larger than they are. Frogs also have the ability to camouflage themselves. Share *Animal Camouflage* and have fun trying to find the creatures hidden in the pictures. Discuss how colors and shapes fool the eye. (*Logical/Mathematical and Visual/Spatial Intelligences*)

Predators of Frogs		
Eggs/Embryos	**Tadpoles**	**Frogs**
leeches beetles other insects salamanders	fish turtles water bugs birds wolf spider bladderwort plant	heron otter weasel owl skunk fox fish garter snake

➤ Figure 1.3. Predators of Frogs

Explore

Have students design frog camouflage pictures by selecting a frog from the book, drawing and coloring it, and carefully cutting it out. Make sure to remind the students of the rules for using scissors safely. Next, have the students design a habitat that provides camouflage for the frog. For example, the shape of the horned frog looks very much like a brown leaf, the markings of the stone toad look like a stone, and the color of the Darwin frog matches green leaves.

Connect

Display the frog pictures and have students try to locate each other's camouflaged frogs. Which were difficult to find? (*Visual/Spatial Intelligence*)

➤ Activity Plan 4: "I Need Food!"—The Frog's Diet

Materials

Short rope (two to three feet in length) that could act as a whip

Engage

Take the rope and swing it in a quick forward whip motion (like a frog's tongue); repeat several times. It is best not to let the students do this.

Elaborate

Explain to the students that the action you demonstrated with the rope is how the frog's tongue moves when it is catching small insects. It sits patiently, waiting for an insect to come within range, then shoots out its long, sticky tongue and grabs the insect. It quickly flips its tongue back into its mouth and swallows the insect. Ask the students to imagine the rope as the tongue of the frog. (Pause and wait expectantly, flip the rope at an imaginary insect, then take a gulping swallow. Repeat several times for emphasis.)

Explore

What else does a frog eat? Have students research and use the board or chart paper to list foods in the frog's diet (crayfish, snails, slugs, worms, fish, and, of course, insects of all kinds). (*Verbal/ Linguistic Intelligence*)

Connect

Ask the students: If the preferred habitat of the frog is a pond, what do our predator/ prey lists for the frog tell us about the pond community? Refocus question: Who are some of the inhabitants of the pond? (See figure 1.3, which lists the predators of the frog; also, refer to the students' list of foods frogs eat.)

➤ Activity Plan 5: "We Live There!"—The Pond Habitat

Materials

Field trip planning to a pond habitat

Fishing waders for you or an adult in the group (This will allow you to gather pond samples without getting too wet.)

Older clothes, sneakers that can get wet (Encourage students to wear these clothes for the field trip.)

Science journals

Scissors

Small jar

Long, thin dowel and a thermometer

String to tie the thermometer to the dowel

Other pond equipment: strainers, scoops, and observation trays made from well-rinsed plastic milk cartons (Separate the cartons into two halves by cutting each carton three inches from the bottom; the bottom half will be the observation tray, the top half will be used to scoop pond water samples; figure 1.4 illustrates this tool.)

The Secret of the Pond, 1991 (video; order from MBG Learning Network, 2025 South Brentwood, Saint Louis, MO 63144; cost: about $35.00)

Mural paper

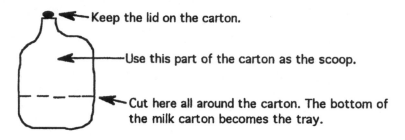

Keep the lid on the carton.

Use this part of the carton as the scoop.

Cut here all around the carton. The bottom of the milk carton becomes the tray.

➤ **Figure 1.4. Milk Carton Scoop**

Engage

Now that you have identified the pond as the frog's main habitat, take a walk to a pond habitat and have the students use their science journals to record observations of other life inhabiting the pond. In the observations described below, you should collect all the samples and take all the readings, to prevent any students falling into the water. (*Bodily/Kinesthetic, Visual/Spatial, Naturalist, and Verbal/Linguistic Intelligences*)

Observation 1

Have students settle far enough from the pond so they can use pages in their science journals to draw overview pictures showing the pond's shape and the plants, grasses, animals, and insects they see.

Observation 2

Divide the class into five or six small groups and use the milk carton scoops to take *surface* pond water samples from a variety of locations on the pond for each group to observe. Have each group place an "S" (for surface water sample) on the overview drawings of the pond to show where their samples are removed from the pond. (Figure 1.5 illustrates this.) Pour the scooped water into the observation trays and let things settle. Have students observe the trays and use their journals to list and describe what they see. Return the water samples to the pond after the observations have been recorded in the journals.

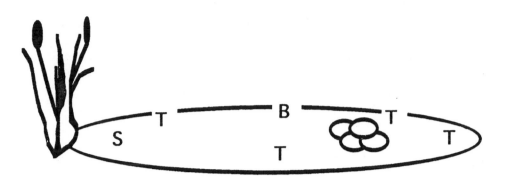

S=Surface water sample analyzed from this location.
B=Mud sample analyzed from this location.
T=Temperature readings.

➤ Figure 1.5. Sampling the Pond

Observation 3

Use the strainer to scoop mud samples from the bottom of the pond in a variety of locations and again have groups mark their pond drawings to show from where samples have been removed. Use the letter "B" to indicate bottom mud samples (see figure 1.5). Have students use small sticks to carefully poke and stir the mud samples and use their journals to record what is found. Return the mud samples to the pond after the observations have been recorded in the journals.

Observation 4

Use the thermometer on the dowel to investigate temperatures at the pond. Measure the temperature at a variety of locations and a variety of depths. Have the students record the temperatures in their journals and mark the pond drawings with the letter "T" for temperature reading samples (see figure 1.5).

Observation 5

Use the dowel to pull a lily pad close to the edge of the pond, use the scissors to snip off one leaf, then scoop the leaf and water underneath and pour the sample into the observation tray. Carefully lift the leaf and show the students what lives under the lily pad. Sprinkle some water on the surface of the lily pad and ask the students to observe how it beads; when the wind blows, the bead of water rolls off the surface. Why is this important to the life of the leaf? (The upper surface of the leaf is filled with tiny pores that allow the leaf to take in carbon dioxide and release oxygen, doing the work of photosynthesis.) Have the students examine the underside of the leaf and ask them: Does it have this same waxy feel? (no) The underside of the leaf doesn't have pores; it provides a home and protection for all kinds of creatures: snails, worms, water bugs, small fishes, water mites, and lots of eggs. Return the lily pad and the water sample to the pond when observations have been completed.

Observation 6

Return to the overview pond drawings and have students select new observation points and add details to their drawings.

Observation 7

Scoop a water sample, pour it into the small jar, and save the sample for observation under the microscope. Later in the classroom, place a small drop of pond water on a slide and cover the slide with another slide. Have the students take turns observing the drop under the microscope. Have them make drawings in their science journals to record their observations. (Algae will be observed; they are one of the basic ingredients for a healthy pond community.) Ask the students why algae are important to the life of the pond. (They provide food for small fishes, insects, and clams, which provide food for larger animals of the pond like turtles and great blue herons; algae make oxygen for the pond; and oxygen supports the life of the pond.)

Elaborate

Return to the classroom to share and discuss the observations from the science journals; then show the video, *The Secret of the Pond.* The video elaborates on characteristics of a pond habitat, identifies common plants and animals of the pond, and explains a food chain. (*Visual/Spatial Intelligence*)

Explore

Ask the students what they have learned. Help students make statements similar to these:

1. The pond is a community of plants and animals. Lots of different plants and animals share the habitat of the pond.

2. Variety is necessary so that each member of the community has what it needs to live and grow. Emphasize the interrelationships of the pond community. Who eats frogs? (snakes, otters, herons) These creatures need frogs to live and grow. What do frogs need to live and grow? (insects, snails, and slugs) What do slugs need to live and grow? (live plants) What do plants need to live and grow? (sun and water) Why are plants important for the life of the pond? (They provide oxygen for the pond.)

Connect

Ask the students to create a mural that illustrates this community. Brainstorm a list of pond inhabitant research topics. (Remind students to think about their science journal observations and what they have learned about the foods frogs eat.) Figure 1.6 lists some suggested topics.

The Pond Community: Topics for Research		
Animals	**Plants**	**Spiders/Insects**
frog duck turtle beaver perch catfish toad salamander raccoon garter snake sandpiper great blue heron snail crayfish otter kingfisher grebe	sedge reed water lily cattail arrowhead duckweed algae bladderwort	dragonfly mayfly water beetle water stick diving beetle water spider mosquito slug backswimmer water strider

➤ Figure 1.6. Topics for Research

Have students gather information they can use to write descriptive paragraphs about the animals or plants. Encourage students to identify how their plants or animals are important to the life of the community. Descriptive paragraphs should follow this format: topic sentence (broad), two to four supporting detail sentences, concluding sentence (see example in figure 1.7). Also, have students identify a scale measurement for the mural. Animals and plants should be drawn/created to that scale.

Raccoon

The raccoon is a carnivore and it has sharp teeth and claws. good for hunting fish and small rodents. If the raccoon is near water, it washes its prey. It's easy to spot because of its black face mask and bushy ringed tail. A hollow in a tree makes a safe home for the raccoon family. Look for the raccoon in the evening because it's a nocturnal animal.

➤ Figure 1.7. Descriptive Paragraph

➤ Activity Plan 6: Mapping Animal Movements— Searching for Hurkle, the Elusive Turtle

Materials

Pond grid (multiple copies, one per student and enough for a practice session and several games) (see activity sheet 1.1)

Engage

Hurkle is a turtle hiding in the pond; biologists want to locate her so they can begin to study her movements and know more about her habitat.

Elaborate

Distribute pond grids and have students practice finding locations in the pond (see figure 1.8).

	1	2	3	4	5	6	7	8	9	10
A										
B										
C										
D										
E										
F										
G										
H										
I										
J										

➤Activity Sheet 1.1. Pond Grid

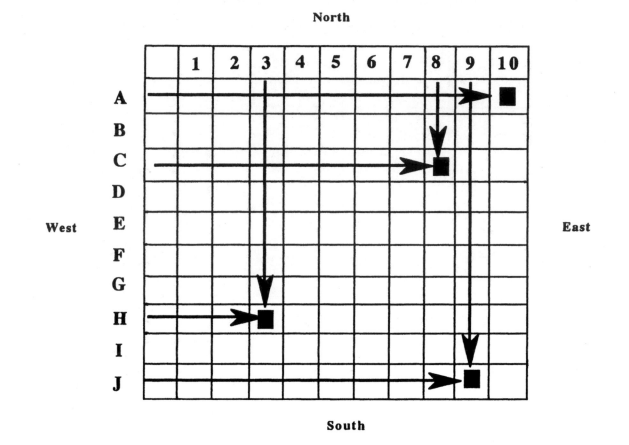

➤ Figure 1.8. Practice Example of Pond Grid

1.   Have students write directions in the margins of the grid sheets: north, south, east, west.

2.   Have them find this location: A log sticks out of the pond at (C, 8) on the grid. They should move horizontally across the grid from the letter C and down, vertically, from the number 8, and then color the box where the two points meet.

3.   Have the students find this location: Southwest of the log, frogs sun on a group of lily pads located at (H, 3). They should move horizontally across the grid from the letter H and move down, vertically, from the number 3, then color the box where the two points meet.

4.   Have them find this location: At the northeast corner of the pond, several boulders edge the water at (A, 10). They should move horizontally across the grid from the letter A and move down, vertically, from the number 10, and color the box where the two points meet.

5.   Finally, have the students find this location: Cattails edge the southeast part of the pond at (J, 9). They will need to move horizontally across the grid from the letter J, then move down, vertically, from the number 9, and then color the box where the two points meet.

Explore

Introduce the search for Hurkle, the turtle. Students will use fresh pond grids and compass direction clues. Follow these directions:

1.   Remind students to write directions on the new pond grids: north, south, east, west.

2.   Choose a leader for the first search.

3.   Without revealing the actual location to the biologists (the rest of the class), the leader decides on a point where Hurkle is hiding, colors that block on the grid, and announces that Hurkle is hiding behind some point on the pond grid. The other players (biologists) need to discover that point.

4.   Biologists take turns predicting coordinates and naming them by ordered pairs, such as (B, 2). The leader responds to each prediction with a clue, telling the biologists in which direction they need to go from their prediction to find Hurkle. For example, if Hurkle is hiding at (F, 5) and the guess is (B, 2), the leader will say, "No, you won't find him at (B, 2), go southeast." Biologists color the square at (B, 2) so they can keep track of where they have already searched, then make a new prediction.

5.   As soon as the leader hears each prediction, he or she should place a finger on the predicted point and then analyze and tell the players in which direction they need to move to find Hurkle. This helps prevent confusion with the directions.

6.   Biologists should continue making predictions until they locate the turtle. (Save the leader's copy of the grid showing the location of Hurkle at this observation time.)

Connect

Explain to the students that once biologists have located an animal (as they did with Hurkle), they use a system for observing short periods or samples of behavior at various intervals and a grid like the one used to map the movements of the animal. The class now has one point in the habitat of Hurkle, the turtle, and will take another sample later in the day to see where Hurkle has traveled. Through these processes biologists can estimate the size of the area used by the animal; identify key locations where the animal spends a lot of time; and determine its food, water, range, and shelter needs. This helps them protect an endangered animal or control a pest species. (*Logical/Mathematical and Visual/Spatial Intelligences*)

Have students continue to take observation samples to map Hurkle's habitat at different times during the day for the duration of the frog unit. After each session, record on a master grid where Hurkle travels. For example, your master grid may show that Hurkle spends time at (C, 2), then moves to (H, 6), then to (A, 10), and so on. The master habitat grid for Hurkle should show these blocks marked in color.

➤ Activity Plan 7: Comparing the Information

Materials

Three large, laminated circles (at least twenty-four inches in diameter) in three colors (These will become floor Venn diagrams.)
Signs for Venn diagram sorting (see figure 1.9)

Engage

Have students draw and cut out small pictures of their pond mural research topics (animals, plants, and insects).

Elaborate

Venn diagrams can help students compare and contrast information. Draw two large overlapping circles on the board and model this process by comparing and contrasting a jet airplane and a hot air balloon. (See figure 1.10.)

Explore

Have students bring the pictures they cut out and gather in a large circle on the floor. In comparing and contrasting in the following exercises, the goal is to look, once again, at the community of the pond to see its variety and how each member's needs are met.

Exercise 1

Place one large circle on the floor with a sign that reads, "I am born in the pond." Have those students whose pictures meet this criterion place their pictures inside the circle; those whose creatures/plants were not born in the pond will place their pictures outside the circle. What variety do students see? Why is the pond necessary for the survival of these creatures and plants? (They would not even be alive without the water of the pond.) (See figure 1.11.)

Exercise 2

Place two large circles on the floor; one circle should hold the sign, "I swim in the pond." The other circle should have a sign that says, "I fly over and around the pond." Start with "I swim in the pond" and have the students determine the pond organisms that belong there. Then have them decide which organisms fit in the "I fly over and around the pond" circle. Several students will probably "have pictures that meet both criteria. Overlap the two circles, and those students whose pictures represent both swimming and flying organisms should place them in the overlapping area. Why is the pond important to these organisms? (food, protection, shelter) (See figure 1.12.)

Text continues on page 21.

I am born in the pond.

I swim in the pond.

I fly over and around the pond.

I live in the pond.

I use the pond.

I weigh over six pounds.

➤ Figure 1.9. Signs for Creating a Venn Diagram

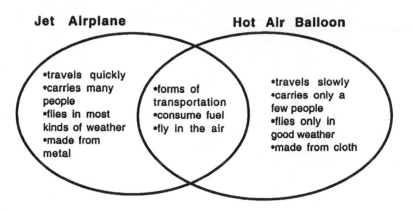

➤ Figure 1.10. Venn Diagram Comparisons: Jets and Hot Air Balloons

➤ Figure 1.11. Venn Diagram Comparisons: Pond Life

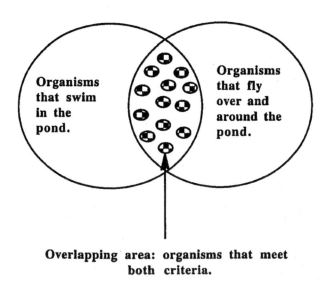

➤ Figure 1.12. Venn Diagram Comparisons: Pond Life, Another Look

Exercise 3

Place three large circles on the floor. The first circle should hold the sign, "I live in the pond." The second circle should have a sign that says, "I use the pond," and the third circle should have a sign saying, "I weigh over six pounds." Starting with circle one, have the students identify the pond organisms that live in the pond. Next, have them identify the organisms that fit the statement, "I use the pond." Overlap the circles and have the students identify the organisms that meet both criteria; move those pictures to the overlapping section. Students should then identify the organisms that weigh over six pounds; overlap this circle with circle one and circle two and identify the organisms that meet all three criteria and that meet any two criteria. (See figure 1.13.)

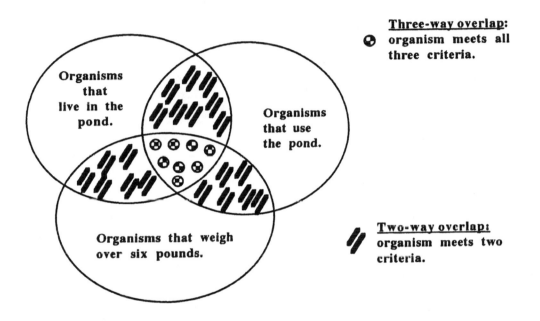

➤ Figure 1.13. Venn Diagram Comparisons: Pond Life, a Third Time

Connect

Some pond community members need the water of the pond for birth and early growth and survival; others swim in the pond in search of food; and still others come to the pond for protection, water, and shelter. Ask the students: What can harm the pond? (garbage, pollution, too many organisms in the pond habitat, not enough oxygen) Scientists call these *limiting factors*, because they limit, or narrow, the life of the community.

2 The Funny Little Woman

Retold by Arlene Mosel
Illustrated by Blair Lent
New York: E. P. Dutton, 1972

Summary

➤ The funny little woman's skill with rice and her ability to laugh bring her unexpected fortune. When the dumpling the funny little woman is making rolls through a crack in the floor, she follows in search of it and is captured by the *oni*. The *oni* teach her to make rice with the magic paddle and she lives with them through the seasons of a year, until longing for her little house gives her courage to leave the *oni* and return to her other life.

Award Year

➤ 1973

Art Information

➤ Illustrated using pen-and-ink line drawings with full-color acrylic glazes.

Curriculum Connections

➤ Geology, with emphasis on these science ideas: Earth materials include solid rocks, soils, and water. The Earth's crust is always changing, through slow process changes like weathering and erosion and through rapid process changes like landslides, earthquakes, and volcanoes.

➤Activity Plan 1: Sharing the Story

Materials

A variety of materials that could demonstrate change:

Pencil and pencil sharpener
Whittling tools (chisel, knife, hammer, soft woodblock)
Glass of milk
Chocolate syrup, spoon
Cup of water and freezer space (check the faculty lounge or the cafeteria)
Fabric and clothing item made from the fabric
Drawing paper
Illustrating materials (crayons, markers, colored pencils)
Caldecott Award poster
Pen and ink (available at art stores)
Acrylic pigment (available at art stores)
Large shallow container of dirt; dirt should be somewhat compact, not loose and crumbly (Save the container for a later lesson on erosion.)

Engage

Write this question on the board: Change: How does it happen? Give students time to think about the question as you create a four-column chart labeled *Before, Tools for Change, After,* and *Speed.* (See figure 2.1.) Use the materials you have gathered to build understanding of change; don't worry about the speed column for now.

1. Show the unsharpened pencil or dull pencil and sharpen it. Ask students to identify the before and after states and the tool used to create the change.

2. Begin with the soft woodblock and use some of the carving tools to begin shaping and changing the wood. Ask the students what information they would place on the chart for this demonstration.

3. Pour milk into the glass, add some chocolate syrup, and use the spoon to quickly mix the two. How would students fill in the chart?

4. Walk to the door of the classroom and open or close it. Ask the students to identify what changes occurred in this example and what the tool for change was.

5. Show the cup of water and ask two students to take it to the freezer. Ask the students to hypothesize about what will happen to the cup of water and what change they would record in the "After" column. Ask them how the change will take place.

6. Display the fabric and the clothing item made from the fabric. Ask students: What was the tool for change?

Change: How does it happen?

Before	Tools for Change	After	Speed
dull or unsharpened pencil	sharpener	sharpened pencil	fast
wood block	hammer, chisel, knife	finished carving	slow
glass of milk	spoon, chocolate syrup	glass of chocolate milk	fast
open or closed door	hand	closed or open door	fast
glass of water	freezer	ice cube	slow
fabric	pattern, scissors, pins, thread, needle, sewing machine	finished item of clothing	slow

➤ Figure 2.1. Change Chart

Ask the students which changes are slow changes and which are rapid changes. Have students analyze the demonstrations and the information in the chart to decide which changes take time and which happen quickly.

Then have students work with partners or in small groups and brainstorm other ideas to demonstrate change. If students are stumped, have them think of cooking changes, animal or plant life cycles, construction projects, and/or household chores. Share the ideas and add the examples to the chart. (*Logical/Mathematical, Bodily/Kinesthetic, and Interpersonal Intelligences*)

Elaborate

Draw the crack in the floor from the opening page of the story (see figure 2.2). Ask the students: What if this crack continued to split and suddenly you found yourself tumbling below ground into an ever-widening space? What would be your reaction? How would you feel? Let's find out how the funny little woman in the story reacts. (*Visual/Spatial Intelligence*)

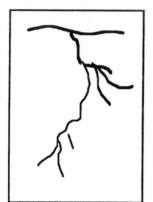

➤ **Figure 2.2. Crack in the Floor**

Explore

Begin the story and read through the fourth page of text, stopping before the *oni* are actually seen by the students. Ask students to imagine how they look and use drawing paper to illustrate them quickly. Show the drawings to see all the different images students have of the *oni*, then return to the story. (*Visual/Spatial Intelligence*)

Connect

Share the Caldecott Award information:

1. As students examine the cover of the book, what is something special that they notice? (gold medal) What is the name of the medal? (Caldecott Award Medal) Why has it been placed on this book? (Some of these answers may be that the illustrations are special, well done, particularly interesting, exciting, and/or unusual.)

2. Discuss the art techniques used in creating the pictures. Return to the beginning of the story and slowly turn the pages as you pose this question to the students: What do you notice about the pattern of the illustrations? (Mr. Lent uses color to focus our attention but leaves a reminder [in pen and ink] of the action continuing above ground; the opening uses full color, but beginning on page 2 Mr. Lent starts the separation in the illustrations, as the colors in the well are removed, then on page 3, as the crack widens and the funny little woman tumbles head over heels, the colors in the tree and the landscape beneath it are removed. This pattern is interrupted for the double-page illustration of the *oni* rowing the funny little woman to the house across the river, but continues on the following page as the funny little woman learns to cook for the *oni*.) What do the pen-and-ink illustrations tell the reader about the time spent with the *oni?* (A year passes.) Acrylic paints were used to add color to the illustrations. Acrylics go on like oil paints but have two advantages: They dry quickly without changing color and they do not darken with time.

3. Ask two student volunteers to search the poster for the year the story won. (Searching the poster helps students become familiar with the many different titles selected for the award.)

From early in the story, we know that the floor of the funny little woman's house is earthen. Display the container of dirt and allow students to pat it to see that it is pretty compact, just like the floor of the house. Discuss these questions with the students: What scientific explanation would you give for the crack in the floor and the widening hole that develops? (Earthquake, sinkhole, shifting foundation, drought) What would be the "tool" that causes the change? Allow speculation, then encourage further investigation and exploration and give students time to develop some explanations. (*Logical/Mathematical and Interpersonal Intelligences*)

➤ Activity Plan 2: Schoolyard Safari— What's in My World?

Materials

Bear hunt rhyme (see figure 2.3)
Plastic baggies (one per student)
Science journals
Pencils
Chart paper
Drawing paper
Illustrating materials (crayons, markers, colored pencils)
A sign that reads: We are all scientists (see figure 2.4)

Text continues on page 31.

Bear Hunt

Let's go on a bear hunt. As you go with us, repeat everything I say and do.

Okay. Are you ready? Let's go on a hear hunt.
Begin walking in place. Stop, put your hand up to shade your eyes as though spying out the land.

I see a wheat field.
Slouch a little and look puzzled.

Can't go over it. Can't go under it.
Smile, straighten up, sound excited.

Let's go through it.
Begin walking and brush palms together back forth making the sound of walking through a wheat field. Then continue walking. Stop, put your hand up to shade your eyes as though you are seeing a bridge.

I see a bridge.
Slouch a little and look puzzled.

Can't go around it. Can't go under it.
Smile, straighten up, sound excited.

Let's go over it.
Begin walking and thump chest with fists. Continue walking.

Scared? Not much.
Stop, put your hand up to shade your eyes as though you are looking at mud.

I see some mud.
Slouch a little and look puzzled.

▶Figure 2.3. Bear Hunt

Can't go over it. Can't go under it.
Smile, straighten up, sound excited.

Let's go through it.
Begin walking and make "shloop, shloop" sounds as though walking through sticky mud. Continue walking. Stop, put your hand to shade your eyes as though seeing a lake.

I see a lake.
Slouch and look puzzled.

Can't go over it. Can't go under it.
Smile, straighten, sound excited.

Let's go through it.
Begin overarm swim stroke. Then shake yourself as if wet and continue walking. Stop and slowly look up into a tree.

I see a tree.
Slouch and look puzzled.

Can't go over it. Can't go under it.
Smile, straighten, sound excited.

Let's go up it.
Pretend to climb a tree. Shade your eyes with one hand and look all around. Speak loudly and with emphasis.

I don't see any bears!
Pretend to climb down the tree and continue walking. Walking slows down. Lean forward as though looking.

I see a cave.

(In a quieter voice...) Can't go over it.

► Figure 2.3. Bear Hunt (*cont.*)

(In almost a whisper...) Can't go under it.

(In a whisper...) Let's go in.
Begin to walk slowly and quietly on tip-toes. Stop and whisper as though afraid.

I see two eyes.
Reach out one hand as though feeling something.

I feel something.
Lean forward again as though you hear a sound.

I hear a growl.
Shout and throw up hands.

It's a BEAR!!!
Immediately reverse all motions.

Run in place.
Climb up the tree and down again.
Swim through the lake and shake yourself as if wet.
"Shloop, shloop" through the mud.
Thump your chest for the bridge
Brush palms together for the wheat field.
Run in place, stop, pretend to slam a door.

Pause and heave a big sigh of relief.

➤ Figure 2.3. Bear Hunt (*cont.*)

We are all scientists.

➤ Figure 2.4. Scientists Sign

Engage

Invite students to participate in the bear hunt (see figure 2.3). (*Bodily/Kinesthetic Intelligence*)

Elaborate

Discuss the senses that helped students on the bear hunt.

1. Eyes to see the wheat field, the bridge, the mud, the lake, the tree, the cave, and the eyes of the bear.

2. Ears to hear the growl of the bear.

3. Touch to feel the wheat, the lake, the tree, and the bear's body (fur, nose, claws, etc.).

Pose these questions: What other senses do we have? (smell and taste) How do these senses help us?

Explain that students will be taking a walk outdoors and using their senses to record and collect information. Students will need the following supplies: a baggy, a science journal, a pencil. As they walk, they should find objects or draw pictures of what they see, hear, touch, and smell. Caution them not to taste anything. (*Bodily/Kinesthetic and Visual/Spatial Intelligences*)

Explore

Return to the classroom and let students sort and share their earth baggies and the pictures in their science journals. Gather students in a large circle on the floor. Invite sharing from the students and have them classify materials from their baggies and their journals. Use chart paper to create a two-column chart labeled "People-Made Materials" and "Earth Materials" (see figure 2.5). (*Logical/Mathematical Intelligence*)

Connect

Pose this question for discussion: What did we learn today? (Our senses help us learn things. Some of the materials and pictures we gathered are made by people and some of the materials come from the Earth.)

People-Made Materials	Earth Materials

➤Figure 2.5. Classifying Materials

Display the sign (see figure 2.4) and have students identify the ways they worked as scientists (observing, collecting, sorting, classifying). Have students close the lesson with one more activity of a scientist: explaining.

Have students select ideas from the "Earth Materials" column and draw pictures explaining why they think these are important. Create a bulletin board titled "The Importance of Earth Materials." (*Visual/Spatial Intelligence*)

➤Activity Plan 3: Soil—What Is It?

Materials

Containers with different types of soil such as clay, compost, sand, garden soil (Available from any garden store or dig from your own yard or the school yard.)
Science journals
Chart paper
Paper plates (small and large)
Paper towels
Magnifying lens (one per student) (Folding magnifiers are available from Delta Education, P.O. Box 3000, Nashua, NH 03061-3000; cost: $2.00 each.)
Toothpicks or bamboo skewers, optional (Available from grocery stores or discount stores.)
Sieves (Invite donations from parents.)

Preparation

Set up soil sampling stations. Place the large container of soil in the center. Spoon small quantities of the soil on small paper plates and surround the large container with the paper plates. (*Note:* Set up enough small paper plates so each student in a group has a place to explore.)

Engage

Display one of the soil containers and pose this question: As you think about our outdoor safari lesson, what tools do you have to explore what is in this container? (senses)

Explain the process for the soil stations:

1. In this lesson you will spend a few minutes at each station.

2. Each of you will look very closely at the soil at each station. You will feel and smell a clump and rub it between your fingers near your ears to hear what it sounds like.

3. Before you leave each station, choose a word to describe the soil, and write it in your science journal.

4. Be sure to wash your hands when you have finished your observations.

Divide the class into groups and assign stations. Set a timer and allow three to five minutes of exploring; then shift stations, repeating the process. Continue until each group has explored each soil station.

Gather the students in a circle and invite them to share the words they wrote describing each soil sample. (gritty, smooth, oozy, cold, wet, crumbly, etc.) Record their responses on chart paper. (*Bodily/Kinesthetic and Verbal/Linguistic Intelligences*)

Elaborate

Have students work with partners to learn more about the garden soil. Spoon samples of the garden soil onto large paper plates, and ask students to use the toothpicks, sieves, and bamboo skewers to examine the soil carefully and list what they find. Circulate as students work to observe their processes, and ask questions to encourage different ways of observing. (*Interpersonal Intelligence*)

Explore

Have each partnership report their findings and create a list of what they found in the soil. (Some ideas to expect include leaves, sticks, sand, little stones, bugs, tiny worms, mud, etc.)

After the list is created, help students identify a basic fact about soil. (Soil is made of many different things.)

Connect

Discuss why soil is important. Have students draw pictures explaining how soil is important and add the pictures to the bulletin board display. (*Visual/Spatial Intelligence*)

➤Activity Plan 4: Rock Collecting— Everyone Needs a Rock

Materials

Four to six rocks for observing (Available from most school supply catalogs. *School Supply* [P.O. Box 1579, Appleton, WI 54912, 888-388-3224] has an inexpensive introductory set of fifteen rocks.) Place each rock on a plate and number the plates. Distribute the plates throughout the classroom.
Activity sheet 2.1 (one per student)
Magnifying glasses
Chart paper

Engage

Slowly share the following clues until most students can identify what you are describing (*Verbal/Linguistic Intelligence*):

> I am found all over the Earth.
> Sometimes I'm smooth, and sometimes I'm rough.
> I can be shiny or dull.
> I have many uses.
> You often see me on buildings.
> Long ago I was used to make arrowheads.
> What am I?

Elaborate

Have students make a "senses" exploration of the rocks. Encourage them to use their observation charts, but don't require information in each box. (*Bodily/Kinesthetic Intelligence*)

Sight: What colors do they see? Is the rock shiny or dull?
Touch: What feeling words describe the rock? (smooth, rough, sharp, heavy, light, cold)
Smell: Smell three parts of the rock. Any surprises?
Sound: What is the sound of the rock when you tap it?

Rock Number	Color	Texture	How Heavy?	How Shiny?	Other Properties
1					
2					
3					
4					
5					
6					

▶ Activity Sheet 2.1. Observing Rocks

Explore

Create a chart comparing the rocks, and ask students to share what they have discovered. (colors, shininess, weight, textures, etc.) (*Logical/Mathematical Intelligence*)

Connect

After the chart is created, help students identify a basic fact about rocks. (There are many kinds of rocks. Rocks have different properties.)

➤Activity Plan 5: Splish, Splash—Discovering with Water!

Materials

Activity sheet 2.2 (one per student)
Large drinking glass
Pitcher of water
Tubs or buckets of water (one for each small group)
Assorted plastic measuring cups and spoons
Assorted objects that float and sink (feather, rock, leaf, cardboard, etc.)
Science journals

Engage

Pour a glass of water for yourself and drink it. Comment on how good it tasted and how thirsty you were. Pose this question to the class: Why do we need water?

Elaborate

Role-play several interactions between water and plants and animals (including humans) and discuss how the scene showed the importance of water to living things.

1. A droopy plant receiving water

2. A rainy day at school

3. A snow day

4. A dog after a long walk in the neighborhood

Water Use Chart   **Name:**   **Day:**

Time: Use:	Time: Use:	Time: Use:
Time: Use:	Time: Use:	Time: Use:
Time: Use:	Time: Use:	Time: Use:

▶ Activity Sheet 2.2. Water Use Chart

Invite students to work with partners or small teams and think of their own examples of interactions between water and plants and animals. (Some examples include: fish swimming, a bouquet of flowers, lemonade, bathing, a raccoon washing its food, boating, swimming, ice skating, washing the dishes or clothes, making coffee, tea, or juice, a birdbath, etc.)

After each partnership or team dramatizes their scene, invite discussion on how the role play showed the importance of water to living things. (*Bodily/Kinesthetic and Interpersonal Intelligences*)

Explore

Divide students into small groups and encourage them to explore the tubs of water to describe some of the properties of water (wet, clear, runs, spills, have to capture it with a container, floats some objects, lets some objects sink).

Gather students in a circle and invite sharing by posing the following question: What did you discover about water? Record the responses and help students discover a basic fact about water. (Water is a liquid.) (*Bodily/Kinesthetic Intelligence*)

Connect

Have students use the water use activity sheet 2.2 to keep track of all the ways they use water in one day. Use the information to develop a class graph and a mural titled "Water Is Important to Earth Because . . . " (*Logical/Mathematical Intelligence*)

➤ Activity Plan 6: Landscape Changes—Introduction

Materials

Selection of rocks: some smooth and weathered, some rough and jagged
Peach or an apple (or another fruit with a central seed core, thick pulp, and thin skin)
Knife
Chart paper or a large sheet of butcher paper (for the web, described below, of forces that build and shape the landscape of Earth's crust)
Science journals (spiral notebooks or other notebooks reserved for science notes and investigations)

Engage

Show the peach or the apple and speculate with students about how the structure of the fruit is an analogy for the structure of the Earth. (The seed is the center of the Earth, the fruit is the next layer of the Earth, and the skin is the outer layer of the Earth.) (*Visual/Spatial Intelligence*)

Elaborate

Slice the fruit in half and look more closely at the analogy. The seed is at the center of the fruit just as the core is the center of the Earth. (Draw a circle to represent the core.) Have students turn to fresh pages in their science journals, date the pages (all scientists date their science notes), and draw as you draw. Figure 2.6 illustrates the analogy.

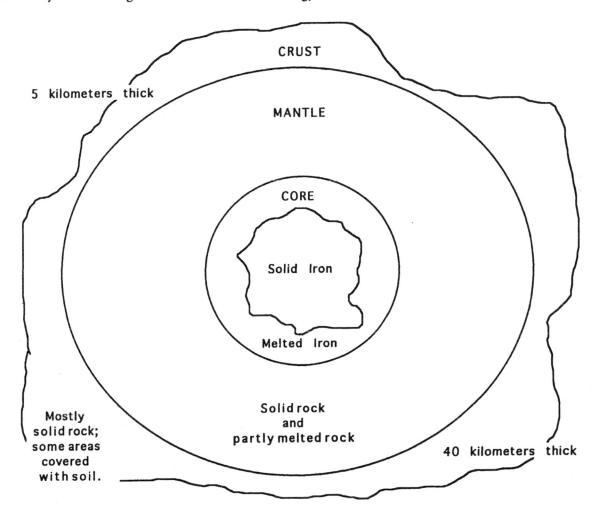

➤ **Figure 2.6. Layers of the Earth**

The core is made of solid iron surrounded by a layer of melted iron. (Add the words *solid iron* and *melted iron* to the drawing, then use orange and yellow chalk or crayons to add color to the melted iron part of the core to represent the heat.)

The fruit of the peach or apple is a good image for thinking about the mantle or next layer of the Earth. This is the thickest part of the fruit, just as the mantle is the thickest part of the Earth. (Draw a larger circle surrounding the core; see figure 2.6.) The mantle is composed of solid rock and partly melted rock. (Add these words to the drawing. Allow time for students to add this information to their journals.)

The crust is the outer layer of the Earth, just as the skin is the outer layer of the fruit. Peel the fruit to demonstrate the thinness and unevenness of the crust. (Draw this uneven circle, being sure to keep it thin; see figure 2.6.) Speculate with students about what causes the unevenness of the crust. (The ocean floor is closer to the mantle, about five kilometers; most land areas average thirty-five kilometers in thickness; mountains add thickness, up to forty kilometers.) Have students complete the drawings in their science journals.

Help students identify nonstandard measurements for these distances: Five kilometers would be a little over three miles, thirty-five kilometers would be about twenty-two miles, forty kilometers would be twenty-five miles. If the school were the starting point, where would students be if they were five kilometers, thirty-five kilometers, and forty kilometers from the school? (*Visual/Spatial Intelligence*)

Explore

Use the chart paper or the butcher paper and have students brainstorm to create a web identifying forces that build and shape the landscape of the crust. Ask them which forces cause slow changes and which cause rapid changes (see figure 2.7). Display the web as a constant visual reminder of the slow and rapid processes that shape the Earth's crust; students may also add to the web as they work in the unit. (*Verbal/Linguistic Intelligence*)

Connect

Introduce the discovery center investigations. These are opportunities for students to explore independent investigations that continue to build understanding of the main science idea, that the Earth's crust is always changing through slow process changes like weathering and erosion and through rapid process changes like landslides, earthquakes, and volcanoes.

1. Decide if students will work individually, with partners, or in small groups; if group work is chosen, decide if students will select their partners or if you will determine the groups.

2. Have students bring their science journals and gather in a large circle; share the details of each investigation.

3. As students hear the details of the investigations, have them note topics they prefer to research.

4. Have students select their investigations.

5. Review the process for working. Students should complete each level of the investigations before continuing to the next level. Emphasize that you will be circulating as they work and will be eager to discuss and share in the results of their investigations; if students are working in groups, emphasize that you will expect to see important jobs for each student at each level of the investigation. For example, in the cave investigation at the knowledge and comprehension levels, one student would research and create a flow chart about sea caves, another would gather information and develop a flow chart about lava caves, and a third would investigate limestone caves and explain their formation through a flow chart. Before continuing to the application level, each partner should share research notes, show the flow chart, and explain what was learned.

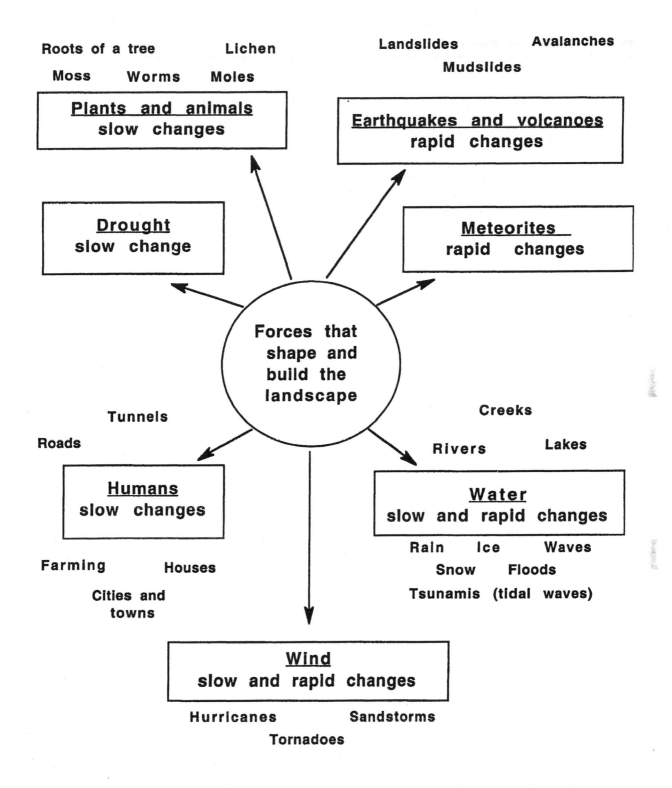

Roots of a tree   Lichen   Landslides   Avalanches

Moss   Worms   Moles   Mudslides

Plants and animals
slow changes

Earthquakes and volcanoes
rapid changes

Drought
slow change

Meteorites
rapid changes

Forces that shape and build the landscape

Tunnels   Creeks

Roads   Rivers   Lakes

Humans
slow changes

Water
slow and rapid changes

Farming   Houses   Rain   Ice   Waves

Cities and towns   Snow   Floods

                                    Tsunamis (tidal waves)

Wind
slow and rapid changes

Hurricanes   Sandstorms

Tornadoes

➤ Figure 2.7. Landscape Web

6. Have students carefully review their chosen investigations and set goals. What will they do first? second? third? If they are working with partners, what will be the job of each partner?

7. Remind students to use their science journals to record information and sketches from each stage of the investigations. (*Interpersonal, Verbal/Linguistic, Bodily/Kinesthetic, Logical/Mathematical, and Visual/Spatial Intelligences*)

8. Create task cards for the students that include instructions for each step of the investigations.

INVESTIGATING CAVES

Knowledge
Begin your investigation of the three kinds of caves: sea, lava, and limestone. Research and take notes about them and how they form.

Comprehension
Make flow charts or diagrams that explain how limestone, sea, and lava caves form.

Application
Work with your team to build a limestone cave. Prepare a short talk about the cave.

Analysis
Meet with a canyon team to compare how a cave forms with how a canyon forms. How are caves and canyons alike and how are they different?

Synthesis
Create a picture that combines your knowledge of canyon formation and cave formation.

INVESTIGATING CANYONS

Knowledge

Begin your investigation of canyons. Research and take notes about how they form and where they are found.

Comprehension

Make a flow chart that illustrates how they form.

Application

Work with your team to build a canyon. Prepare a short talk about the canyon.

Analysis

Meet with a cave team to compare how a canyon forms with how a cave forms. How are caves and canyons alike and how are they different?

Synthesis

Create a picture that combines your knowledge of canyon formation and cave formation.

INVESTIGATING VOLCANOES

Knowledge

Begin your investigation of volcanoes by researching and taking notes on how they form and erupt.

Comprehension

Make a flow chart or diagram that explains how they happen.

Application

Work with your team to build a volcano. Prepare a talk about how volcanoes form and erupt.

Analysis

Meet with an earthquake team to compare volcanoes and earthquakes. How are they alike and how are they different?

Synthesis

Create a picture that combines your knowledge of how and where volcanoes and earthquakes form.

➤ Activity Plan 7: Landscape Changes—Frost Wedging

Materials

Containers of ice (one per student partnership; clear plastic disposable cups will work; be sure the containers are full enough so that the water cracks them when it freezes)

Containers of water (one per student partnership; use container identical to the ones holding the ice, and fill them with the same amount of water as you placed in the cups that you froze)

Marbles placed in the freezer (one per student partnership; clear, uncracked glass)

Water and a pan

Hot plate

Spoon

Science journals

Engage

Distribute the containers of frozen water and freshwater, and have students speculate about why the frozen containers cracked. Explain that both cups held the same amount of water. (Frozen water expands beyond its original volume and exerts pressure on the container, eventually cracking it.) (*Logical/Mathematical Intelligence*)

Elaborate

Bring the water to a boil. Remove the marbles from the freezer and distribute them to the students so they can see that they are uncracked and can feel how cold they are. Have students speculate about what will happen when the marbles are placed in the boiling water. (Responses you might hear: They will crack. Nothing will happen. They will get hot.) Slowly place the marbles in the boiling water and let them boil for two minutes. Turn off the heat, remove the marbles, let them cool, and return them to the students. Speculate about why the marbles cracked. (The sudden temperature change made the marbles' molecules expand suddenly.) (*Logical/Mathematical Intelligence*)

Explore

Write "Weathering" on the board and use the frozen water cups and the cracked marbles to speculate about and discuss how frozen water and temperature extremes shape and change the landscape of the Earth's crust. (Water flows into cracks and spaces in rocks and freezes when the temperatures turn cold; the ice makes the cracks and spaces in the rocks widen, and over the years continued freezing and thawing breaks the rocks apart. Temperature extremes also cause weathering; the sun heats the rocks during the day, and night temperatures rapidly cool the rocks, causing a similar effect as the cracking of the marbles.) Ask students to think about these questions:

Why is frost wedging not a force in polar or tropic regions of the world? (Frost wedging requires temperature variations from above to below freezing.)

Is frost wedging a slow process change or a rapid process change? (Slow, because it takes years.)

What areas of the world are particularly subject to daily extremes in temperature? (deserts)

How do temperature extremes change the landscape of the desert? (The heat and cold cause the continuous expansion and contraction of rocks, resulting in the cracking noticed in the marble. Eventually the rocks will break into smaller pieces.)

Are these changes slow process or rapid process changes? (slow)

Connect

Take a walk on the school grounds and the surrounding neighborhood to search for examples of weathering caused by frost wedging and temperature extremes. Share and discuss the examples of weathering that students discovered on their walk. Ask students to define weathering. Refocus question: What is weathering? (the process of breaking rocks into smaller pieces)

Have students use their science journals to record their understanding about frost wedging, the results of rapid temperature changes, and the definition of weathering, then continue to work in discovery center investigations. Remind them to date each day's entries. Circulate to discuss and assess progress. (*Intrapersonal and Bodily/Kinesthetic Intelligences*)

➤ Activity Plan 8: Landscape Changes— People, Plants, and Animals

Materials

Open space for seed and animal burrowing dramatizations
Drawing paper
Illustrating materials (crayons, markers, colored pencils, water colors, pen and ink)
Science journals

Engage

Have students dramatize the following scene; model the process with them.

1. Imagine yourself as a seed held in the beak of a bird soaring in the sky when suddenly you feel yourself floating to the ground and settling on rocky ground. (Students should stand without shoes, pretend to float, then land on the floor, crouching and tightly curling their bodies, feet scrunched together with toes pointing straight ahead.)

2. This rocky ground seems a most unlikely place to grow, but soon you are pushed along the rock by spring rains until you find yourself caught in a crack of the rock, surrounded by just enough soil for growing. As the sun warms your coat, you un-curl a little and begin to sprout roots, pushing and straining to widen the crack in the rock and find a toehold. (Students should roll to a new spot, crouch again, spread their feet slightly, and push them as though they are cracking and widening the rock.)

3. More rain washes over you and you slowly sprout through the leaves and rock bits and soil collected in the crack in the rock; your roots push more deeply into the crack, searching for room to spread and grow; your stem pushes taller. (Students should slowly extend a hand as though they are sprouting, then spread their feet a little more, then begin to stand.)

4. Sun and rain help you grow tall and strong, your roots expand and push deeper. (Students should slowly rise to standing position, with both arms extended above their heads, feet spread a little more.)

5. The years pass and you grow taller and your roots grow stronger and bigger, cracking and crumbling the rock around you. (Students should spread their feet even wider and reach taller with their arms.) (*Bodily/Kinesthetic Intelligence*)

This dramatization illustrates another example of weathering, plants breaking and crumbling the surrounding rock. Mention cracked, pushed-up sidewalks with tree roots poking through the concrete, and dandelion plants and other weeds sprouting from cracks in driveways, walls, and roadway medians, as examples from the city.

Elaborate

Ask the students: How can some animals weather the landscape? (As they dig tunnels and burrow into the ground, they loosen rocks and soil, allowing air and water to move deeper into the ground.) Dramatize this process of weathering caused by burrowing animals: Twelve students will be the tunnel, two students will be burrowing animals, and the rest of the students will be the air and water.

1. Create two rows of students, six students in each row; students should stand with shoulders and right feet touching and feet comfortably apart; each student partnership should stand about one foot behind the other (see figure 2.8).

2. The two students selected to be burrowing animals should get down on their hands and knees and approach the front of the tunnel; as the first burrowing animal's head touches the right legs of the "tunnel," "tunnel" students should shift their right legs toward their left legs, opening a space for the animals to burrow.

3. Air and water students should follow the burrowing animals, pushing the tunnel wider ("tunnel" students should shift their right legs again and widen the space of the tunnel).

4. Have the students repeat the cycle of animals burrowing followed by air and water; the tunnel widens each time the air and water swoosh through it.

Students standing side by side in two rows, shoulders and right feet touching.

➤ Figure 2.8. Burrowing Animals Exercise

Worms, moles, and prairie dogs are examples of burrowing animals that weather the landscape. Ask the students if the effects of burrowing are slow process changes or rapid process changes. (slow) (*Bodily/Kinesthetic Intelligence*)

Explore

Ask the students how people weather the landscape. (digging tunnels, leveling the land, constructing buildings, farming, blasting to build roads, dredging channels for waterways, breaking rock and stone for the outer walls of houses, creating projects like Mt. Rushmore in South Dakota and Stone Mountain in Georgia) Have students work with partners to illustrate examples of how people weather the landscape. If they are stumped for ideas, suggest thinking about the neighborhoods where they live, changes in the city or a vacation spot, development in the countryside, and changes that occur on a farm. (*Visual/Spatial Intelligence*)

Connect

Have students share their pictures and use their science journals to summarize the three forces that weather the landscape that were introduced in this lesson. (plants, animals, and humans)

Have students continue to work on discovery center investigations. Remind them to date their science journals for each day's notes. Circulate to discuss and assess progress.

➤ Activity Plan 9: Landscape Changes—Abrasion

Materials

Hand lotion

Sandpaper in various degrees of smoothness (A small package from a hardware or home improvement store can provide the variety needed.)

Scraps of wood (Contact a lumber, home improvement, carpentry, or woodworking store and ask for scrap donations.)

Science journals (Students will illustrate and describe examples of weathering seen on the field trip.)

Field trip planning to a rocky area for hiking and observing

Engage

Give students a dollop of hand lotion and have them rub their hands until the cream is completely absorbed. Have them describe what happened. (As the students continued to rub, the cream smoothed their skin, softened rough or scaly places, changed callused areas, changed dry spots.)

Have students use the sandpaper to smooth the scraps of wood. Ask them what happens to the wood scraps as they continue to sand them. (They smooth out, change shape and size, and lose uneven spots.) (*Bodily/Kinesthetic Intelligence*)

Elaborate

Ask the students what forces in nature act like the sandpaper. Refocus question: What forces continually rub the landscape? (waves, wind blowing sand against rocks, and rocks in a river or creek rubbing the bottom and sides of the riverbed or creek bed) Ask students what the outcome of this constant rubbing or abrasion is. (Surfaces become smooth, rocks crack, the shape changes, the landscape is carved.)

Explore

Take a hike with students in a rocky area and have them use their science journals to describe and illustrate examples of weathering (frost wedging, temperature changes, plants, animals, humans, abrasion). (*Bodily/Kinesthetic Intelligence*)

Connect

Gather in a large circle and have students report examples of weathering they observed during the hike. Have students draw before and after pictures on a chart by folding pieces of drawing paper in half, then labeling the left side "now" and the right side "one hundred years from now" (see figure 2.9). Have them select examples of weathering and draw the examples as they are now, then imagine the landscapes one hundred years from now and draw pictures of the new landscapes. Display the drawings. (*Visual/Spatial Intelligence*)

Now	One Hundred Years From Now

➤ Figure 2.9. Weathering Comparison Chart

Have students continue to work in discovery center investigations. Remind students to date their science journal entries. Circulate to discuss and assess progress.

➤Activity Plan 10: Landscape Changes— Chemical Weathering

Materials

Rusted nail
Bottle of carbonated water and two other carbonated drinks
Small cups (one per student)
Glass of water
Straw
Rock samples (limestone, marble, slate, granite, basalt)
Chalk (one piece per student partnership)
Small plates (one per student partnership)
Eyedroppers (one per student partnership)
Rubber gloves
Science journals
Student products from the discovery centers (Have students begin presenting their "application level" products, the limestone caves, the canyons, the earthquake wave demonstrations, and the volcanoes.)

Engage

Have students take sheets of notebook paper and weather them by tearing, cutting, folding, crumpling, stomping on, and/or poking holes in them. When they smooth out their paper, it is still recognizable as paper. The landscape weathering discussed so far illustrated how these forces change the sizes and shapes of rocks but not the contents of rocks. Chemical weathering changes the minerals that make up the rocks. Explore this with the students. (*Bodily/Kinesthetic Intelligence*)

Elaborate

Display the bottle of carbonated water, the carbonated drinks, and the glass of water. Have students breathe deeply and exhale several times. Ask them what is released into the air when humans exhale. (carbon dioxide) Show the glass of water, breathe deeply, and exhale through the straw into the glass. Explain that carbonated water (or carbonic acid) is formed when carbon dioxide gases dissolve in rainwater or groundwater. When we drink these carbonated drinks, we are drinking carbonic acid. Open and pour the carbonated drinks and have students take sips. Ask students to describe what they see and what they taste. (They might say it *fizzes, bubbles, tingles, "burns" if you drink it too quickly*.) Ask them what the properties of an acid are. (dissolves; eats away at a substance)

Explore

Carbonic acid can slowly dissolve some kinds of rocks. Display the rocks, explaining, for example, that limestone rock has a high concentration of the mineral calcite and is particularly affected by the carbonic acid. Have student volunteers use the eyedropper to drip some carbonated water onto the rock samples. Ask students what changes would begin to happen over time in the limestone as this chemical weathering process continues. (As the acid seeps through the limestone, it erodes the calcite, making holes.) Ask them what the end result would be. (a cave)

Have student partnerships investigate chemical weathering using the chalk and the carbonated water. Explain that students should place the chalk on small plates and use the eyedroppers to drip carbonated water onto the chalk. Remind them to record all the steps they follow and to make drawings of the results of each step. For example, one team might drip five drops on the chalk and draw a picture showing the immediate results. They might draw additional results at five minute intervals. They might add drops of water after fifteen minutes of observation and continue to record the results. (*Logical/Mathematical and Interpersonal Intelligences*)

Connect

Invite students to share their chalk investigations and results. Show the rusted nail and speculate about why it rusted. (The nail is made of iron; when it is exposed to oxygen in moist air, it forms iron oxide or rust and begins to crumble.) Rocks that contain iron can rust in this same way and slowly crumble into red soil. Ask students why this is an example of chemical weathering. (The weathering changed the minerals in the rocks.) Have students date their science journals and record notes about chemical weathering. (*Logical/Mathematical Intelligence*)

Have some students present their models and give talks about the models. Then continue to work in discovery center investigations. Circulate to discuss and assess progress.

➤ Activity Plan 11: Landscape Changes—Erosion

Materials

Two outdoor locations: a sidewalk location close to a water faucet and an outdoor work area
Broom
Hose attached to outdoor faucet
Spray nozzle attachment for hose
Gravel, leaves, twigs, and/or grass clippings
Chart paper
Containers of dirt (one per small group; shallow, heavy-duty cardboard boxes work well)
Old spoons
Pitchers of water (for each group)
Measuring cups (for each group)
Large rocks

Science journals
Student products from the discovery centers (Have students continue presenting
their "application-level" products: the limestone caves, the canyons, the earthquake wave demonstrations, and the volcanoes.)

Engage

Spread the gravel, leaves, twigs, and grass clippings on the sidewalk. Ask the students
what forces could be used to clear the sidewalk of the debris. (wind, broom, feet, water) Divide the
class into groups representing each of the forces: wind (several students), broom (two students), feet
(several students), water from the hose (two students), water from the hose when the spray nozzle is
attached (two students).

Elaborate

Have each group work at clearing the sidewalk. Wind students should crouch and blow
together on the count of three, broom students take turns sweeping, feet students shuffle through the
debris, water (without spray attachment) students aim the hose at the debris, and water (with spray
attachment set at greatest pressure) students aim the hose at the debris. Analyze the effects of each
force. Ask the students which force cleared the sidewalk most effectively. (The hose with the spray
nozzle attached should have cleared the sidewalk.) (*Bodily/Kinesthetic Intelligence*)

Explore

Continue developing understanding of erosion. Write this statement on the chart paper:
"Erosion is the movement of weathered materials to new places." Explain to the students that one of
the most powerful erosion forces is water, as you discovered with the hose experiment; water is a force
that carries loose materials (debris on the sidewalk or weathered rock) away to a new place. The debris
moved more quickly when you increased the speed of the flowing water.

Divide students into small groups (two or three students per group), distribute the supplies
(containers of dirt, spoons, pitchers of water, measuring cups, rocks), and have students investigate the
effects of water on dirt. Use the chart paper to brainstorm questions, such as the following, to investigate:

1. What happens to the land when water moves slowly?

2. What happens when we elevate the container and pour water?

3. What happens when water meets an obstacle like a rock?

4. What happens if we dig a ditch?

Remind students to use their science journals to make detailed notes about their investigations, including the steps they follow, the results of each step, and the conclusions they form. Circulate
as students work, posing questions and reviewing their science journal entries. (*Logical/Mathematical
and Interpersonal Intelligences*)

Connect

Have students share their erosion investigations, and as a class draw conclusions about the effects of water on land. Some of their conclusions may be that:

1. Erosion moves weathered materials to new places.

2. Wind can cause erosion, but in most places water is the biggest cause of erosion.

3. Elevation (or the steepness of the land) can increase erosion. If the land is steep, the water runs faster. When the water runs faster, it can move more weathered materials or sediment.

4. The amount of water that flows can increase erosion. More weathered material moves when there is more water.

Have students present their models and their talks (from the "application level" of the discovery center investigations), then continue working on analysis and synthesis products.

➤ Activity Plan 12: Landscape Changes—Rapid Processes

Materials

Transparency of figure 2.6 (Layers of the Earth)
"Surface Features." *Windows on Science, Earth Science 2, Primary Science* (Available from Optical Data Corporation, 30 Technology Dr., Warren NJ 07059; cost: about $500.)
Laser disk player
Television

Engage

Use the transparency to review the layers of the Earth and their compositions (core, mantle, crust), and look again at the web listing the forces that shape the Earth's crust (figure 2.7). Ask students what some of the rapid process changes are (earthquakes, volcanoes, mud slides, floods, hurricanes) and why these are rapid process changes. (because they can quickly change the look of the landscape, buckling and breaking apart the crust, downing trees, carving new water channels, changing the shape of a mountain)

Elaborate

Use the *Windows on Science* images for the lessons on volcanoes and earthquakes to show and discuss the changes in the Earth's crust caused by these rapid process events. (*Visual/Spatial Intelligence*)

Explore

Have students search books, magazines, encyclopedias, and computer resources to find pictures of landscape changes caused by mud slides, landslides, avalanches, sandstorms, earthquakes, and volcanoes. (*Visual/Spatial Intelligence*)

Connect

Have students share the pictures and explain the landscape changes that have occurred.

➤ Culminating Activity Plan

Materials

Student products (analysis and synthesis stages) from the discovery center investigations

Engage

Review the forces that shape and build landscapes: slow process forces like weathering (forces that change rocks) and erosion (forces that move weathered rocks); rapid process forces (earthquakes, volcanoes, landslides, and avalanches).

Elaborate

Create comparison charts on the board and have students or student teams share information from their discovery center analysis comparisons (see figure 2.10).

Explore

Have students share and explain their discovery center synthesis products.

Comparisons

Caves	Canyons	Earthquakes	Volcanoes
Slow process	Slow process	Rapid process	Rapid process
Sea caves: caused by the pounding of ocean waves. Lava caves: caused when lava hardens on the surface, but hot lava still flows underneath. Limestone caves: caused by chemical weathering when carbonic acid erodes limestone, water drains away, and air enters the open space.	Caused by water erosion. Form in mountain and plateau areas. Many have a river or stream at the bottom.	Caused when plates bump into each other, move apart, grind past each other, or slide over each other. Happen at plate boundaries.	Caused when magma and gases push up from inside the Earth and explode through the crust. Happen at plate boundaries and hot spots (cracks in the mantle).

▶ Figure 2.10. Slow and Rapid Processes Compared

Connect

Now that discovery center work is complete, have students make generalizations that demonstrate their understanding. Ask them: What are the forces that shape and build the landscape of Earth? Generalizations can be tentative, abstract, accurate, or qualified. A tentative statement might be: "Many caves are formed when acid rain or groundwater seeps through limestone rock." (Tentative generalizations use words such as *many, some, often,* and *seldom.*) An abstract statement might be: "Landforms (such as caves and canyons and mountains) are formed because of a slow process of weathering." (Abstract generalizations use broad terms such as *landforms,* rather than specific terms such as *cave, river,* or *island.*) An accurate statement says something that is true, that can be supported with evidence, such as: "Most volcanoes and earthquakes cause rapid process changes in the Earth's crust." A qualifying statement uses limiting words: *if . . . then, when . . . then.* An example of a qualifying statement is: "When the land is steep and water runs faster and moves more weathered materials or sediment, then erosion happens more quickly."

3 Make Way for Ducklings

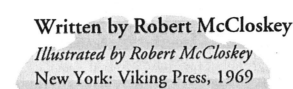

Written by Robert McCloskey
Illustrated by Robert McCloskey
New York: Viking Press, 1969

Summary

➤ Mr. and Mrs. Mallard were looking for a place to live. They tried an island in the pond of the Public Garden but the danger from bicycles was too great, they flew over Beacon Hill and the State House but couldn't see a likely place, and they tried Louisburg Square but it didn't have water. At last they located a perfect spot near the Charles River and just in time for the arrival of their eight ducklings. Training the ducklings, trips to gather peanuts from Michael the policeman, and a return journey to the Public Garden keep the new parents very busy.

Award Year

➤ 1970

Art Information

➤ Illustrated using lithographic pencils on stone.

Curriculum Connections

➤ Ducks, with emphasis on this science idea: An animal's habitat should provide what the animal needs to stay alive and live and grow; it's the place where the animal's needs for air, food, water, space, and shelter must be met.

➤Activity Plan 1: Sharing the Story

Materials

    Drawing paper
    Pencils
    Chart paper (use it to create the cluster web; save the web)
    Caldecott Award poster
    Grease crayon (available at art stores)
    Limestone rock
    Soft cloth
    Cup of water

Engage

Have students draw large circles and use the circles to illustrate their understanding of the life cycle of a duck (see figure 3.1). Share and display circle illustrations. Begin a cluster web about ducks that illustrates life cycles, structures, adaptations, and interdependence (see figure 3.2). (*Visual/ Spatial Intelligence*)

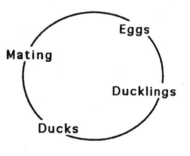

➤**Figure 3.1. Duck Life Cycle**

Elaborate

Read the story and invite student participation in reciting the names of the ducklings. Pose these questions before beginning: What important structures of ducks help them adapt to their environment? How does the story illustrate interdependence?

Explore

Discuss the story. As the story developed we saw that it took several tries before Mr. and Mrs. Mallard found a place to build their nest. Ask the students: What were their criteria? Once they chose the island and the ducklings hatched, why didn't they remain on the island in the Charles River? What would you look for if you were looking for a new home? Why didn't the cars stop for Mrs. Mallard and her ducklings? How else might the ducks have crossed the street? Which parts of the story seem real? Which parts are probably make-believe?

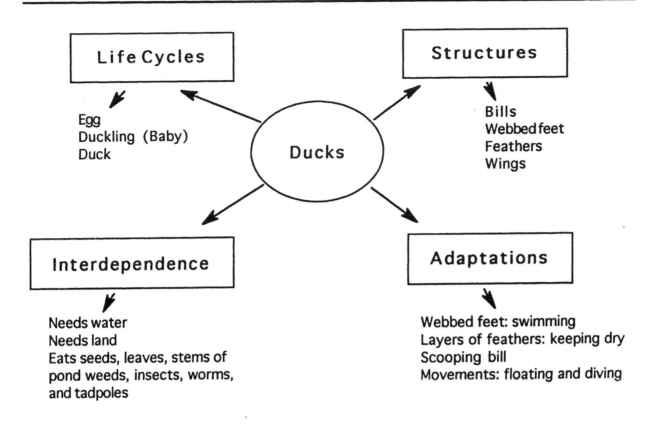

➤ Figure 3.2. Duck Cluster Web

How did the story illustrate the habitat needs of ducks (water, source of food, protected from danger)? What structures help ducks adapt to their environment? Add any new responses to the web.

It is interesting to look at all the illustrations of the ducks. Mr. McCloskey was able to draw them so realistically because he purchased two mallards and kept them in his apartment in New York City to closely observe them in motion. For weeks he followed them around the apartment on his hands and knees with his sketchbook, watching them move and even swim in his bathtub. He later acquired six baby ducklings and made hundreds of sketches in the same way.

Connect

Share the Caldecott Award information:

1. As students examine the cover of the book, ask them what special thing they notice. (gold medal) Ask them the name of the medal. (Caldecott Award Medal) Ask why it has been placed on this book. (Some answers may be: The illustrations are special, well done, particularly interesting, exciting, and/or unusual.)

2. Discuss the art techniques used in creating the pictures. Lithography on stone is an interesting technique. The artist uses the grease crayon to draw an image on the stone, then applies a fixative to help the stone hold more water. (Draw a simple shape on the stone and pretend to add the fixative with the soft cloth.) Water is poured over the stone and absorbed except where the grease crayon image is drawn. (Pour water over the stone.) Ink is rolled onto the surface of the rock; it only adheres to the grease crayon image, not the wet stone. The stone is placed in a press, paper is applied, the press is squeezed, and the image appears on the paper. (Pretend to roll ink onto the surface of the rock, place the rock upside down on an illustration in the book, pretend to press, remove the rock, and show the illustration in the book.) That's how Mr. McCloskey created the illustrations. (Browse the pictures, noticing the details and the light and dark areas in many of the figures.)

3. Ask two student volunteers to search the poster for the year the story won. (Searching the poster helps students become familiar with the many different titles selected for the award.)

Close the story sharing by dividing the class into teams of four and having a duck walk relay race. (*Bodily/Kinesthetic Intelligence*)

➤ Activity Plan 2: Animal Habitats— Working As Scientists

In working as scientists, students observe and ask questions, predict answers (hypothesize), test ideas (experiment), record the results, and think about and explain the results.

Materials

Field trip planning: Find a field trip opportunity in which students can observe animals in habitats (zoos, parks, aquariums, or local nature areas like wetlands, forests, etc.)
Science journals
Illustrating materials (colored pencils, crayons, markers)

Engage

Have students use their science journals to draw pictures of their homes and the immediate surroundings where they live. When the drawings are complete, have the students label the parts of the drawings that provide what they need to stay alive and live and grow. (*Visual/Spatial Intelligence*)
The items labeled should be answers to questions like the following:

What is their source for air? (They should label the sky around the home.)

What are their sources for water? (City systems, wells: Have students draw pipes going into their homes, or wells, and label these sources for water.)

What are their sources for food? (Kitchens, grocery stores, restaurants, gardens: Have students label the kitchens of their houses.)

What is their shelter? (Have students label their homes.)

What is their space in the house? (Bedrooms: Have students label the parts of their houses where their bedrooms are located; discuss whether they share that space and if so, how they manage the sharing.)

What are their roles/jobs in the home? (Discuss chores and responsibilities.)

Elaborate

Discuss the habitat needs of ducks. What did the class learn from the story? (The mallards wanted to be near water and needed sources of food, protection from danger, and nest-building materials.) Have students use new pages in their science journals to draw pictures of the mallards in their island home near the Charles River. Label the parts of the drawing for sources of air (the surrounding sky), water (the Charles River), food (grasses, plants, insects and animals of the island and the water, peanuts from Michael), shelter (nest), and space (the island). (*Visual/Spatial Intelligence*)

Explore

Take the field trip and have students use their science journals to draw pictures of habitats of animals in the field trip location. Remind them to label the habitat pictures for sources of air, food, water, space, and shelter. (*Bodily/Kinesthetic and Visual/Spatial Intelligences*)

Connect

Explain that the class will be housing some animals for observation for the next few weeks and that students need to design appropriate habitats to house the animals. Divide the class into teams and have each team select one animal, investigate the habitat needs of that animal, and record the information in their science journals. (*Verbal/Linguistic and Interpersonal Intelligences*)

➤ Activity Plan 3: Animal Observations

Materials

Science journals

Selection of containers that can be used to create habitats (large jars, old aquariums, small animal cages, plastic swimming pools; possible sources for the containers are donations from families, flea markets, and contributions from other teachers)

Rubber gloves

Animals for observation (lizard, a hamster or gerbil, fish, hermit crabs, frogs or toads, worms, and crickets; check local pet stores)

Activity sheet 3.1, Observation Chart (seven to ten copies per team)

Animal Observation

Date_____   What We See_____

	Morning Observation Comments	Afternoon Observation Comments
Food		
Sleep		
Activity		
Other		

▶ Activity Sheet 3.1. Observation Chart

Engage

Have students return to the information they have gathered about the habitat needs of the animals they have been investigating, analyze the information, and develop plans for building the habitats. (*Logical/Mathematical, Bodily/Kinesthetic, Visual/Spatial, and Interpersonal Intelligences*)

1. The first step in the process is to share the information researched by each team member. Have students spend some time sharing what they have learned about the habitat needs of the animals. After team members have shared their research information, encourage students to address this question: How might we construct a habitat that best meets these needs?

2. The answer to this question completes the second step in the process: hypothesizing or proposing a solution. Have students work with their team members to plan the habitats. Circulate and listen to their planning and help list the materials and supplies that will be needed.

3. The third step in the investigation is to build the habitats.

Elaborate

Have students construct the animal habitats.

Explore

Discuss care and responsibility behaviors needed for safe animal handling. (wearing rubber gloves, gentle handling, clean drinking water, daily food)

Arrange to have the animals in the classroom, place them in their habitats, and encourage students to observe their activities and habits. Once the animals are in their habitats, move onto the next step of the process: observing and recording information about the animals as they live in their habitats. Have students decide what information they would like to record about the animals (such as sleep and eating habits and activity descriptions). Have student teams place multiple copies of the animal observation sheets (activity sheet 3.1) in notebooks (one notebook per animal), date the sheets, and begin to record their observations. Each day students should take care of the animals and record their observations. Set aside time each day to discuss the observations.

Connect

After seven to ten days, have children read and discuss all the information on the animals' eating habits, sleeping patterns, and activities. How would students evaluate the ability of the habitat structures they constructed to provide air, food, water, space, and shelter for each animal? (*Logical/Mathematical and Verbal/Linguistic Intelligences*)

➤Activity Plan 4: Like Water off a Duck's Back!

Materials

Outer feathers (one per student partnership) (*Note*: Feathers are available from most hobby and craft stores; they also can be ordered from Delta Education, P.O. Box 915, Hudson, NH 03051, 800-258-1302 or Nasco, 901 Janesville Ave., Fort Atkinson, WI, 800-558-9595; cost: about $1.00 per package of five.)

Vegetable oil (Each partnership will need a small container of oil; one tablespoon should be enough.)

Paper towels

Cups of water

Science journals

Engage

Ask the students to imagine swimming all day without getting cold or wet. Can they explain how a duck does it? Ask them to speculate about how ducks keep their feathers from becoming waterlogged. (*Logical/Mathematical Intelligence*)

Elaborate

Investigate duck feathers to see how they work. Distribute two duck feathers and containers of oil and water to each student partnership. Pose these questions: What happens to the feather when it is splashed with water? What happens to the feather when it is coated with oil and then splashed with water? Remind students to work carefully and be thorough in recording their observations and steps. Have students use their science journals to describe what happens. (The water should soak an uncoated feather and bead and roll off a feather coated with oil.)

Explore

Ask the students: Why does the water react this way? How would this help the duck? (Oil and water don't mix, so oil on the feathers would keep the outer feathers from becoming waterlogged.)

Connect

The duck has two layers of feathers: light fluffy down feathers and outer feathers like the ones the students coated with oil. The duck uses its broad beak to coat these outer feathers with oil. The oil comes from a gland at the base of the tail, and the duck gets oil from the gland on its beak, then runs the beak through the feathers, thoroughly coating them with this protective film of oil. The duck repeats this action several times a day.

➤Activity Plan 5: I Need Space

Materials

Glass of water
Potting soil
Lettuce or cress seeds
Potting containers (One per student; seek donations from a garden center, or have
    students bring plastic or clay pots from home.)
Water
Science journals

Engage

Ask for two student volunteers and have them face each other, then move closer to each other until their toes are touching. Discuss space needs. How did the students feel when someone stood that close? How did they want to react?

Display the glass of water and have students think about this situation. Because of a drought this glass of water is all that is available each day to the family of rabbits who live nearby. Ask the students how the rabbits would respond to the lack of water. (move away, die, lose weight, not produce other rabbits)

Elaborate

Ask the students why space is important to animals. (Too many animals crowd the availability of shelter and reduce the amount of food and water.)

Explore

Explore the need for space with plants. Have students carefully pour the potting soil into the potting containers, smoothing and watering it, and planting the seeds. After planting the seeds, have students hypothesize how many plants can successfully live in the space of the container. Place the containers in a sunny location and watch the seeds sprout and grow. Have students record the number of seeds that sprout and continue to observe what happens as the seedlings grow. (Some should begin to yellow and wilt because of the lack of space.)

Connect

Ask students why space is an important habitat consideration for plants. (Crowding takes away adequate water and light.)

➤Activity Plan 6: Ducks for a Day— Working As Writers

Materials

In working as writers, students will gather ideas (prewriting strategies), write first drafts expressing their ideas (rough drafting), conference with other writers to review and make changes in their first drafts (revising and editing), and share their finished work (publishing).

Activity Sheet 3.2, Plotline Brainstorming Sheet (multiple copies)
Activity Sheet 3.3, Duck Shape (Multiple copies; students may choose to draw their own.)
Illustrating materials (crayons, colored pencils)

Engage

Share the writing choices and allow students to choose between the story and the poem. Review the steps of the writing process and emphasize that each step is important and leads to a wonderful, exciting published copy. Tell them, for example:

> We know that the subjects of the poem and the story are ducks. In completing the prewrite brainstorming for the poem, think of all the interesting facts you know about ducks and their behaviors: how they move, what they eat, what sounds they make, how they spend their time, where they live, what they look like in bright sunshine or in the rain.
>
> When you think about the story, what do you imagine? Are the ducks attending duck school, like the one led by Mrs. Mallard in *Make Way for Ducklings*, or has a duck come to our classroom? Imagine what would happen. How would a duck behave? Use the plotline brainstorming sheet as your prewrite preparation (activity sheet 3.2; see figure 3.3 for a sample plotline of a story idea.)

Elaborate

Once the students have several ideas listed, they can begin their poems or stories. In their rough drafts, they don't need to worry about how it sounds, spelling, or punctuation. Encourage them to just begin writing, using the ideas from their lists. As they think about their poems, you can help them imagine themselves as the observers by saying:

> You are taking a walk. You hear a noise, investigate, and see some ducks. You want your audience to see what you see and feel the pleasure and joy you have experienced. Show us what you see. (See figure 3.4 for a sample poem.)

Text continues on page 70.

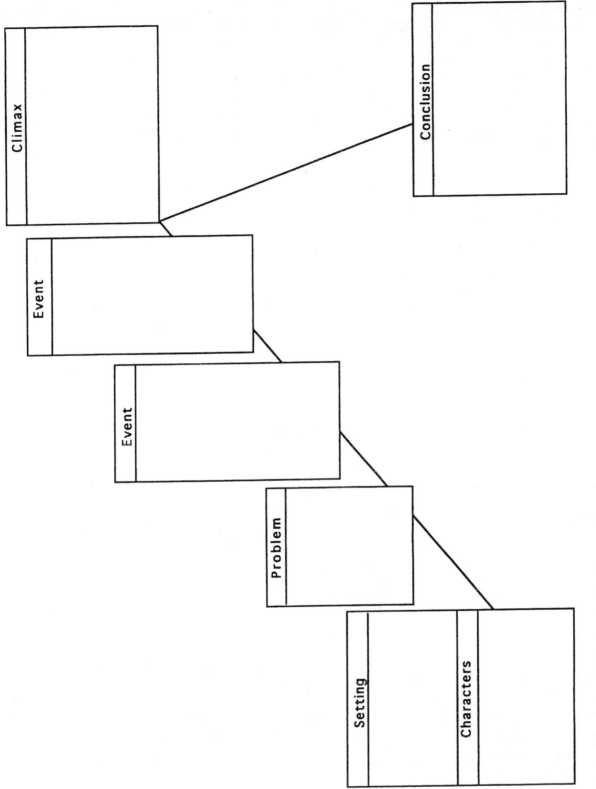

▶ Activity Sheet 3.2. Plotline Brainstorming Sheet

▶ Activity Sheet 3.3. Duck Shape

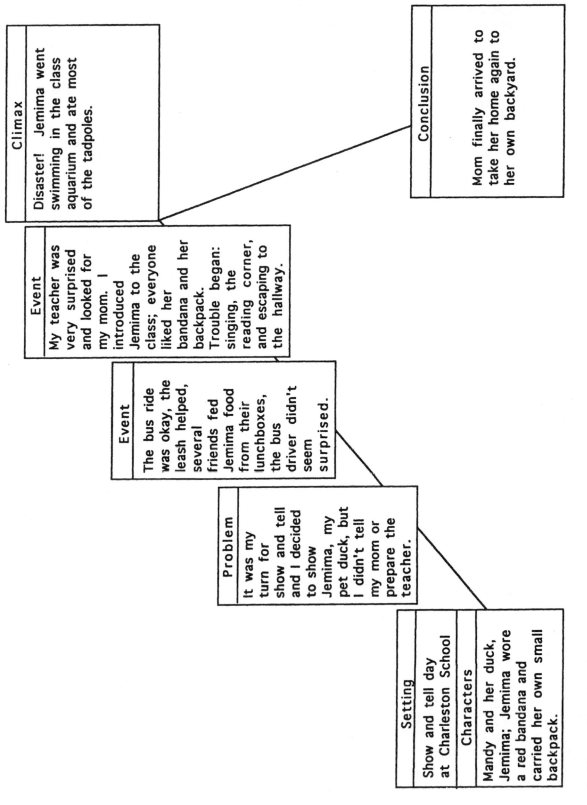

Climax		Conclusion
Disaster! Jemima went swimming in the class aquarium and ate most of the tadpoles.		Mom finally arrived to take her home again to her own backyard.

Event

My teacher was very surprised and looked for my mom. I introduced Jemima to the class; everyone liked her bandana and her backpack. Trouble began: singing, the reading corner, and escaping to the hallway.

Event

The bus ride was okay, the leash helped, several friends fed Jemima food from their lunchboxes, the bus driver didn't seem surprised.

Problem

It was my turn for show and tell and I decided to show Jemima, my pet duck, but I didn't tell my mom or prepare the teacher.

Setting

Show and tell day at Charleston School

Characters

Mandy and her duck, Jemima; Jemima wore a red bandana and carried her own small backpack.

▶ Figure 3.3. Sample Plotline (Duck Story)

Next, ask them to look at their plotlines and think about how they can add details to this information so that the reader will really understand what happened when the ducks went to school. Refocus question: How will you add to the information on your plotline?

➤ Figure 3.4. Sample Duck Poem

> Dip, dip, and search,
> dabbling ducks go bottoms up
> for tasty seeds and leaves.
> Gliding smoothly
> across the sun-sparkled pond,
> glossy green heads dazzling,
> fading from sight
> In the tall reeds along the shore.

Explore

When your students have their rough drafts completed, they should read through them and begin to make changes. Have them share their writing with you or a classmate, read it again, and make more changes. Remind them that the thesaurus can help improve their word choices. For example, if they use "waddle" several times to describe the movement of the duck, they may want some variety; a search of the thesaurus suggests "sway" or "swing." Maybe several sentences didn't make sense to a classmate. Now is the time for revising those sentences or phrases so that they are clearer. In revising the first draft, the goal is to make every word and sentence show something to the reader.

Another step in changing the rough draft happens while the students edit their work. Have them work with a partner to check each other's spelling, punctuation, and capitalization.

Publishing! Now your students are ready for the final copy. The poem will become a shape poem; they can draw their own duck shape or use activity sheet 3.3. Have them carefully write their poems around the outside of the duck, adding color and a surrounding setting (see figure 3.5). For the story, they may write their final copies in their most readable handwriting or use the computer. They can also add illustrations for the story.

Connect

Have students begin working on their writing projects. Circulate as they work through the steps of the writing process, giving encouragement and support. Figure 3.6 summarizes the process and is a good reminder to place on the chalkboard or overhead projector.

Text continues on page 74.

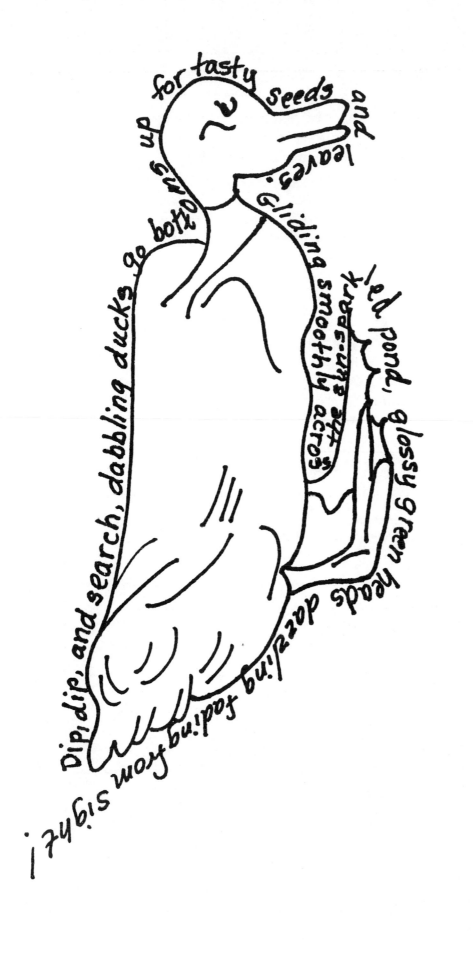

▶ Figure 3.5. Duck Shape Poem

Working As Writers	
Prewrite brainstorming	What are all the interesting facts you know about ducks and their behaviors?: movements, diet, sounds, daily activities, habitat, colors and shape
Rough Drafting	The poem: Show us what you see! Imagine yourself as the observer. You've been taking a walk, hear a noise, investigate and see some ducks.
	The story: What do you imagine? Are the ducks attending duck school like the one led by Mrs. Mallard in *Make Way for Ducklings* or has a duck come to your classroom? *Don't worry about how it sounds or about spelling or punctuation.*
Revising	Read and make changes. Conference and make changes. Don't forget the thesaurus.
Editing	Check that spelling, punctuation, and capitalization. Work with a partner.
Publishing	Hurray! Final Copies Poem: Write the poem around a duck shape, add color and a surrounding setting.
	Story: Write your final copy in your most readable handwriting, or you may use the computer to type your poem.

➤ Figure 3.6. Working As Writers

DUCK POETRY

Use the writing process (prewrite, rough draft, revision, editing, publishing) to write a poem about a duck. As the prewrite, make a list of twenty words and phrases that describe ducks and their sounds and actions. Using the words and phrases from the list, write the first draft of your poem, then read it and begin to make changes. Share the poem with a peer and discuss words and phrases that might be improved. Make the revision changes and work with a partner to make editing corrections (spelling, punctuation, and capitalization). Publish your poem by turning it into a shape poem; use the duck shape in the center or draw your own duck and write your poem around the outside of the duck, then add color and a surrounding setting. (*Verbal/Linguistic Intelligence*)

DUCK STORY

Use the writing process (prewrite, rough draft, revision, editing, publishing) to create a story about ducks going to school. As the prewrite, complete the plot line brainstorming sheet: Imagine and describe the setting for the school, identify the problem, briefly describe two events in the story that lead to the climax, describe the climax or most exciting part, and finish the plotline by explaining the conclusion. Using the words and phrases from the plotline, write the first draft of your story, then read it and begin to make changes. Share the story with a peer and discuss words and phrases that might be improved. Make the revision changes and work with a partner to make editing corrections (spelling, punctuation, and capitalization). Make a final copy of your story, either writing it in your best handwriting or typing it on the computer. Illustrate your story. (*Verbal/Linguistic Intelligence*)

➤Activity Plan 7: Ducks for a Day—Working As Artists

In working as artists, students observe and imagine, sketch and plan, gather materials, and create art pieces.

Materials

Make Way for Ducklings by Robert McCloskey
Colored chalk
Tissues
Colored pencils
Drawing paper
Old magazines (for cutting)
Scissors

Engage

As a class, look again at the illustrations in the book and remind students that McCloskey purchased two mallard ducks and kept them in his apartment so he could closely observe them in motion. The observation sketches prepared him for creating the book's published pictures.

Elaborate

Share the art choices and allow students to choose between the chalk drawing and the collage. Review the steps for working as an artist and emphasize that each step is important and leads to a wonderful art piece. For example, ask students:

1. What's the first step in creating a piece of art? (Students will probably respond with "get an idea.") Some good ways to get ideas are to observe and imagine. That's what you will be doing in these two art projects. If you are creating the chalk picture, look at pictures of ducks and imagine yourself in a setting with ducks. What do you see? If you are creating the collage, read about what ducks eat, imagine yourself as a duck, and dream of all the tasty foods you like to eat.

2. Once you have an idea, sketch and plan how it will look.

3. The third step is gathering materials. Chalk picture artists will need chalk, tissues, and colored pencils; collage artists will need pictures from magazines, hand-drawn pictures, and real objects.

4. Now you are ready to create your art piece. Look at your sketch and begin to create!

Explore

Have students choose their art projects and begin the process of creating. Figure 3.7 gives a visual reminder of the steps and can be displayed on the board or an overhead projector.

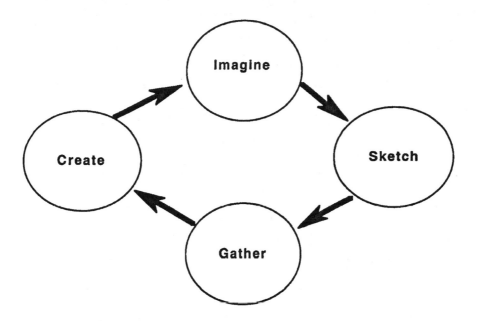

➤ Figure 3.7. Working As Artists

Connect

Display the published art pieces and tour the display. Invite each student to speak briefly about his or her art piece.

DUCK DRAWINGS

Imagine a duck scene, then use a pencil to lightly sketch the picture. Gather your supplies—colored chalk, tissues, and drawing paper—and begin to create the scene. An interesting way to add a feather effect to your ducks is to use several shades of chalk and fill in the duck shape with very small lines. Then use a piece of tissue paper to softly blend the colors together so they look like feathers. (*Visual/Spatial Intelligence*)

DUCKS AND THEIR FAVORITE FOODS

Imagine yourself as a duck and dream of all the tasty foods you like to eat. Plan a collage showing the foods, then use real foods, pictures cut from magazines, and hand-drawn pictures to make a collage showing foods that ducks like to eat. (*Visual/Spatial Intelligence*)

➤ Activity Plan 8: Ducks for a Day— Working As Performers

In working as performers, students gather ideas and information, write or plan (scripts, songs, jokes, dance routines), gather materials (props, costumes, scenery, musical instruments), rehearse, and perform.

Materials

Selection of simple musical instruments (drums, keyboard, horns, rattles)
Ranger Rick magazine, November 1986

Engage

Reprise the duck walk from the opening lesson.

Elaborate

Share the performance choices and allow students to choose between the rap and the skit. Review the steps for working as performers and emphasize that each step is important and leads to a wonderful production. Tell students, for example:

1. The first step in working as a performer is to gather ideas and information. There are lots of interesting duck words; you and your partner will investigate the words, choose five that you really like, and use them in your original song. Duck parade performers, your job is to read about the real-life duck parade that happens in Indonesia. Be sure to take notes as you read.

2. Once you have the information you need, script planning and song planning come next. Scripts need actions and words; songs need tunes and words.

3. The third step is gathering props and costumes and designing and creating any scenery you might need.

4. Then rehearse! rehearse! rehearse! It's no fun for the audience if you are unprepared or you can't be heard.

5. Performance day! Are you ready? Before setting a performance deadline, we will work for a while, then discuss how the performances are developing before we decide when to perform.

Explore

Help students divide into groups and begin the process of working as performers.

Connect

Schedule a performance day and perform the raps and skits. Figure 3.8 provides a visual reminder of the steps and can be displayed on the chalkboard or an overhead projector.

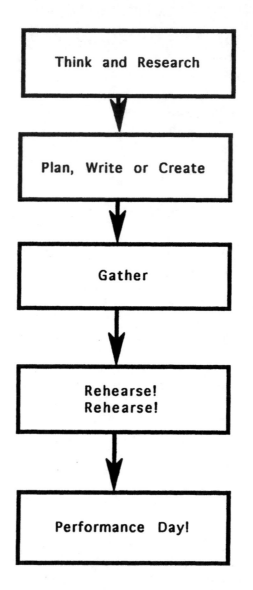

➤ Figure 3.8. Working As Performers

DUCK WORDS GALORE

Work with a partner to investigate duck words. Create a song or a rap sharing the meanings of the words. Use at least five of these words: *duck hawk, duckbill, ducking stool, duckpins, duckweed, duckling, duck blind, duckboard, ducks and drakes, duck soup, ducktail,* or *ducky.* Choose instruments and design movements for your song. REHEARSE, REHEARSE, and REHEARSE AGAIN! Perform the song for the class. (*Musical/Rhythmic Intelligence*)

THE DUCK PARADE

Have you ever seen a real live duck parade? Find out about the duck parade in Bali, Indonesia. (*Hint*: Use *Ranger Rick* magazine, November 1986, pages 16–17.) Create a skit that demonstrates the facts of the duck parade; design scenery, props, and costumes if you need them. REHEARSE, REHEARSE, and REHEARSE AGAIN! Perform the skit for the class. (*Bodily/Kinesthetic Intelligence*)

4   *Many Moons*

Written by James Thurber
Illustrated by Louis Slobodkin
New York: Harcourt, Brace, 1943, 1971

Summary

➤ Princess Lenore falls ill from a surfeit of raspberry tarts and takes to her bed; when questioned about what will make her well, she replies that she wants the moon. Her father places this demand before his council of wise men: the Lord High Chamberlain, the Royal Wizard, and the Royal Mathematician; they give one explanation after another why her wish cannot be granted. In a rage the king calls the Court Jester, who wisely consults Princess Lenore and soon finds a way to grant her wish.

Award Year

➤ 1944

Art Information

➤ Illustrated using pen and ink and washes of reds, blues, and yellows.

Curriculum Connections

➤ Space, with emphasis on this science idea: Exploring and studying the Earth's moon, a small slice of the universe, help scientists hypothesize to better understand the universe: how it's put together, how it works, and where humans fit in it.

➤Activity Plan 1: Sharing the Story

Materials

Moon music (The public library is a good source; some suggestions are "Blue Moon," "By the Light of the Silvery Moon," "Fly Me to the Moon," "It's Only a Paper Moon," and "Moon River.")

"The Moon's the North Wind's Cookie" by Vachel Lindsay, in *Favorite Poems Old and New*, selected by Helen Ferris (Garden City, NY: Doubleday, 1957)

Signs from the story (see figure 4.1); mount each rectangle on separate sheets of construction paper

Paper and pencil (to record proposed solutions)

Caldecott Award poster

Water-soluble pen and ink (available from art stores)

Watercolors: red, blue, yellow (available from art stores)

Paintbrush

Small cup of water

Drawing paper sheet

Engage

Play moon music; recite the familiar Mother Goose rhyme "The Cat and the Fiddle," and read the poem "The Moon's the North Wind's Cookie" by Vachel Lindsay. (*Musical/Rhythmic and Verbal/Linguistic Intelligences*)

Elaborate

Ask the students what other stories/ideas about the moon come to mind. (Some ideas you might expect are: There's a man in the moon, the moon is made of green cheese, full moons cause wild behaviors, the harvest moon tells farmers when to harvest.)

Introduce the story, and as you share the responses from each court advisor, display the story signs (figure 4.1). Read the story up to the page on which the Court Jester interviews the princess to ask what she thinks is the size, distance, and composition of the moon. (The page begins, "It will be very easy to get the moon for you . . ." and ends with the Princess saying, "Oh, it's made of gold, of course, silly.") Place a bookmark at that page, pause (as though you are in the king's shoes), and pose this question to the students: How would you solve the king's problem?

Explore

Use the creative problem-solving process with students to explore solutions to the problem. (*Logical/Mathematical Intelligence*)

From the Lord High Chamberlain...

Too far: 35,000 miles away
Too big: it's bigger than the room where the
Princess lies.
Besides, it's made of molten copper.

From the Royal Wizard...

Too far: 150,000 miles away
Too big: it's twice as big as this palace.
Besides, it's made of green cheese.

From the Royal Mathematician...

Too far: 300,000 miles away
Too big: it's half the size of this kingdom.
Besides, it's round and flat like a coin, it's made of
asbestos, and it's pasted on the sky.

Princess Lenore said...

Not that far: sometimes it gets caught in the top
branches of the big tree outside my window.
Not that big: it's just a little smaller than my
thumbnail.
And, it's made of gold!

➤ Figure 4.1. *Many Moons* Signs

Fact Finding

What are the facts of the situation? Refocus questions: Who can help? What skills and resources are available for the solution? (See figure 4.2 for examples of possible responses.)

Facts of the Situation
1. The King will try anything to solve the problem; because he is a king, he has lots of resources in the kingdom that can be used to solve the problem.
2. The Lord High Chamberlain is good at acquiring things: animals, jewels, minerals, and people.
3. The Royal Wizard is good at magic: golden touch, cloak of invisibility, potions, magic wands, and medical cures.
4. The Royal Mathematician can solve problems involving numbers.
5. The advisers are not willing to "get the moon."
6. The Court Jester is practical, plays the lute, and listens well.
7. According to the Princess, the moon is made of gold, it's a little smaller than her thumbnail, and it's not as high as the big tree outside her window.

➤ Figure 4.2. Facts of the Situation

Problem Finding

What will be the problem statement? Refocus questions: Why is the king sad and what does Princess Lenore need? Expect a problem statement similar to this one: How might the Court Jester bring the moon to Princess Lenore and thus make her well again?

Idea Finding

What are the solutions? Have students work in groups of four to brainstorm solution ideas. Roles for group brainstorming include recorder (writes the proposed solution), presenter (shares the proposed solution with the class), encourager (keeps the group focused and on task), and timekeeper (watches the time). (See figure 4.3. This is a good reminder to place on the chalkboard or overhead projector.)

Roles for Group Work	
Recorder	Writes the proposed solution.
Presenter	Shares the proposed solution with the class.
Encourager	Keeps the group focused and on task.
Timekeeper	Watches the time.

➤ Figure 4.3. Group Work Roles

Solution Finding

Make a creative problem-solving solution grid on the board (see figure 4.4) and have presenters share proposed solutions; summarize and record their solutions on the board. Have students brainstorm criteria to rate the solutions; some answers you might expect from the students include overcomes distance problem, solves size problem, addresses composition problem, brings the moon to the princess, uses resources from the kingdom. Use a scale of one to five (one is "not an effective solution"; five is "an effective solution") to rate the proposed solutions.

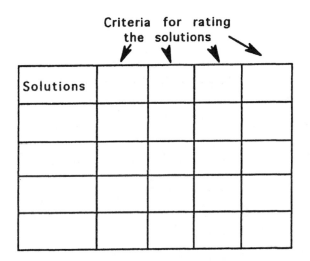

➤ Figure 4.4. Creative Problem-Solving Grid

Acceptance Finding

Read the rest of the story to hear Mr. Thurber's solution.

Connect

Share the Caldecott Award information:

1. As students examine the cover of the book, ask them what special thing they notice. (gold medal) Ask them the name of the medal. (Caldecott Award Medal) Ask them why it has been placed on this book. (Expect some of these answers: The illustrations are special, well done, particularly interesting, exciting, and/or unusual.)

2. Discuss the art techniques used in creating the pictures. The illustrations are cartoonlike and started with pen and ink for the figures and shapes; watercolor paints added the colors we see, and a technique called wash shadowed and smudged some of the pen-and-ink lines. (Browse the book to show the pen-and-ink shapes, then look again to show the addition of color and examples of wash. For example, on the second page of the story, the ink of the bedposts, the underside of the canopy, and the back of the bed have been washed with water, causing shadowing of many of the lines; then additions of yellow and diluted red watercolors have been made.)

3. Ask two student volunteers to search the poster for the year the story won. (Searching the poster helps students become familiar with the many different titles selected for the award.)

➤ Activity Plan 2: Facts About the Moon

Materials

Moon music from Activity Plan 1: Sharing the Story
Signs from Activity Plan 1: Sharing the Story (see figure 4.1)
Moon research chart; enlarge this on an oversized sheet of butcher paper and allow
    enough space so students can record all of their research information (see activity
    sheet 4.1)

Note: If the distinction between what scientists know (column one) and what they think they know (column two) is too challenging for students, just create a three-column chart and record the research information in a column entitled "What We Have Learned About the Moon."

What Scientists Know About the Moon	What Scientists Think They Know	What Scientists Want to Know	What I Would Like to Know

▶ Activity Sheet 4.1. Research Chart

Engage

Reprise the moon music and analyze the facts from the advisors and Princess Lenore (see figure 4.1). Ask students which statements they think are true statements. (Write "yes, true statement" or "no, not true statement" next to each.)

Ask the students: What are tools for learning about the moon? Refocus question: How do astronomers (space scientists) study the moon? (Possible answers include telescopes, telescopes in satellites orbiting the Earth's atmosphere, space probes, manned travel to the moon.) (*Musical/Rhythmic and Logical/Mathematical Intelligences*)

Elaborate

Have students brainstorm questions for research; record their questions on the moon research chart (in the fourth column). Review the rest of the moon research chart and emphasize and explain the two ways in which scientists record information: what they know about the moon (e.g., through years of observation and study, scientists have determined that the same side of the moon always faces the Earth) and what they think they know (e.g., by studying the moon rocks brought to Earth by *Apollo* astronauts and lots of photographs and other data, scientists have developed a theory or explanation about how the moon formed; one theory suggests that the moon formed about 4.6 billion years ago when Earth collided with a Mars-sized object).

Explore

Ask two students to research the truth of the statements from the advisors in the story. (Just how far is the moon, what is its size, and what is its composition?) Divide the brainstormed questions among the rest of the students and have them conduct research to answer the questions, then analyze the research information to decide which column is the best place to record the research results. (As students are researching, circulate and evaluate with them whether the information they are finding is a fact or a theory/proposed explanation.)

When the chart is filled, review the information that has been discovered, then review the accuracy of the statements from the advisors. (The distance from Earth is 239,000 miles, so the Royal Mathematician comes closest, although he overestimates by 61,000 miles; the diameter of the moon is 2,160 miles, so the Royal Mathematician might be right again if half the size of the kingdom equals the diameter measurement, but we don't know for sure; all of the advisors are wrong when describing the composition.)

Have students focus on the third column; return to the resources and find something that scientists still want to know about the moon and record this information in the third column. (*Verbal/Linguistic and Logical/Mathematical Intelligences*)

Connect

Set up a calendar for recording moon observations. Encourage students to pick a time to observe the sky each evening and to draw the shape of the moon and record location information. Each day during the unit, record the students' shape observations and discuss the location movements to note changes.

Introduce the discovery centers:

1. Read the details of the three choices and encourage students to identify the investigations that most interest them.

2. Have students select their investigations and brainstorm how they will proceed. Suggested steps include:

   • Read and research.

   • Take notes.

   • Prepare the product.

   • Conference with peers and/or the teacher to improve the product.

   • Revise and improve the product.

   • Rehearse the presentation.

   • Present the product.

3. Have students work on their investigations. Circulate to hear progress and help with any needs that may arise.

A SHADOW ON THE MOON

Investigate lunar eclipses and solar eclipses and demonstrate how they happen. Use your demonstration to explain the differences. When will the next ones take place? (*Bodily/Kinesthetic and Interpersonal Intelligences*)

TRAVELING TO THE MOON

Pretend to be an astronaut who traveled on one of the *Apollo* missions to the moon. Research your journey and write a letter to a first-grade classroom describing your experiences: What did you see? What did you do? What did you eat? What equipment did you use? (*Verbal/Linguistic Intelligence*)

CHANGES IN THE MOON

Work with a small group of students to create a skit to dramatize the phases of the moon: new moon, crescent moon, first-quarter moon, gibbous moon, full moon. How does the moon look in each phase? Also be sure to explain why there are phases of the moon. (*Interpersonal and Bodily/Kinesthetic Intelligences*)

➤Activity Plan 3: The Moon Is a Satellite

Materials

Open area in the classroom or on the playground
Three signs, reading "Earth," "Sun," and "Moon" (see figure 4.5)
Three safety pins

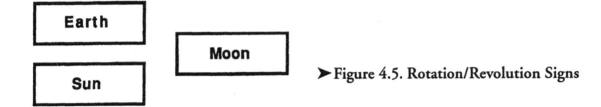

➤Figure 4.5. Rotation/Revolution Signs

Engage

Have students explore rotating movement and revolving movement. (*Bodily/Kinesthetic Intelligence*)

Rotation

Have students stand at least an arm's length from each other and rotate (spin) their bodies several times.

Revolution

Have the students form a large circle, standing shoulder to shoulder, then select a student volunteer to stand at the center of the circle. Ask students to start revolving (circling in unison) around the student in the center of the circle.

Elaborate

Have students discuss the two movements and identify the main difference between them. (In revolving, the students needed an object about which to revolve; the rotation movement did not require another object.) Now have students combine the two movements.

Rotation/Revolution

Have students keep the shape of the large circle, but expand it so they are standing at least an arm's length from each other. Keep a student at the center point of the circle, then have the rest of the students begin rotating (slowly) and revolving at the same time.

Although we can't feel them, these are the movements of Earth. The Earth rotates once every twenty-four hours and takes 365 days (one year) to revolve once around the sun. Earth's revolution around the sun is called an orbit, because that is the path it takes as it moves around the sun.

Explore

The moon also follows this pattern of movement, but instead of moving around the sun it moves around the Earth. Its path (orbit) around the Earth takes twenty-seven days and eight hours. Select two student volunteers to be the Earth and the Earth's moon. (Pin the Earth sign to the front of the shirt of the "Earth" student and pin the moon sign to the front of the shirt of the "moon" student; emphasize that because of the rotation of the moon we always see the same side of the moon.) Demonstrate the revolution movement of the Earth's moon by having the "moon" face the "Earth" and slowly begin revolving. When the "moon" has returned to its starting point in the orbit, twenty-seven days and eight hours have passed.

The rotation of the Earth's moon is harder to understand because the same side of the moon is always facing us. The moon turns just enough each day to keep one side always facing the Earth; its day lasts almost a month, with two weeks of daylight and two weeks of nighttime.

Connect

The Earth's moon is a satellite of the Earth. Ask the students if from the demonstrations they can determine a definition of a satellite. (It's an object in space that moves around another object.) Ask them how the Earth is a satellite. (It moves around the sun.)

Have students work on their discovery center investigations. Circulate to hear progress and help with any needs that may arise.

➤ Activity Plan 4: How Much Does It Weigh?— The Effects of Gravity

Materials

Small, soft ball that can be tossed indoors
Math manipulatives (Student partnerships will use the cubes to count weights of animals; depending on the weight of the animal, some students may wish to count by ones or fives, so gather two kinds of cubes, either different colors, with each color representing a different weight—i.e., red would be one pound and blue would be five pounds—or different sizes, with each size representing the different weights.)
Animal weight chart (see figure 4.6)
Scale

Weighing In			
Animal	Weight on Earth	Weight on the Moon	Non-standard Measurement
koala	30 pounds		
gorilla	200 pounds		
leopard	100 pounds		
wolf	80 pounds		
harbor seal	150 pounds		
woodchuck	12 pounds		
porcupine	40 pounds		
armadillo	15 pounds		
salmon	25 pounds		
baby elephant	200 pounds		
jackrabbit	8 pounds		
badger	20 pounds		
ostrich	300 pounds		
pronghorn deer	140 pounds		
snapping turtle	50 pounds		

➤ Figure 4.6. Animal Weight Chart

Engage

Toss the ball into the air and ask students why it doesn't keep going. (Gravity pulls it back.) (*Bodily/Kinesthetic Intelligence*)

Elaborate

Gravity is a force of attraction between everything in the universe. Objects with more mass pull more strongly than objects with less mass. Gravity keeps the planets orbiting the sun; it makes the Earth a planet where we can live because it keeps the atmosphere from moving away. The atmosphere provides the air we breathe, it protects us from the sun's rays, and it evens the temperatures we experience. Because the gravity of the moon is six times less than Earth's gravity, it isn't strong enough to "keep" an atmosphere. That's why astronauts wear space suits, to give them the air they need to breathe. Also, because the moon's gravity is less than Earth, humans weigh less, jump higher, carry heavier rocks, and throw farther.

Explore

Ask the students to imagine the life of an animal on the moon and ask them: How much would it weigh? How would its movements change? (These are imagining and thinking questions and really don't need answers.) Then explore the weight differences.

Have student partnerships select animals from the weight chart (figure 4.6) and use math cubes to figure out the weights of the animals on the moon. Record the weights and then calculate nonstandard measurements; for example, if a koala bear weighs thirty pounds on Earth, it would weigh five pounds on the moon, which is the weight of a small bag of sugar, or if a woodchuck weighs twelve pounds on Earth, it will weigh two pounds on the moon, or the same as eight sticks of butter.

If students are uncertain about how to proceed, discuss the steps for solving the problem with them, as follows:

1. Count the weight of the animal. For example, if the gorilla weighs 200 pounds and you use the 5-pound cubes, you should count by fives and accumulate forty cubes; if the wolf weighs 80 pounds, you can count eighty 1-pound cubes or by fives to accumulate sixteen 5-pound cubes.

2. Divide the weight by six. The gravity of the moon is six times less than the gravity of Earth, so you should sort your cubes into six piles that are as evenly divided as possible.

3. Determine the weight of the animal on the moon. Count the cubes in one pile and record this weight on the animal weight chart (figure 4.6). If the cubes divide evenly into six piles, you would record an exact number (e.g., two pounds or twenty pounds); if the cubes did not divide evenly, you would add the word "about" to the weight measurement (e.g., about three pounds or about forty pounds).

4. Identify a nonstandard measurement. Use the scale to compare the weight on the moon to a nonstandard measurement that helps you understand the moon weight measurement.

Connect

Review the chart to share the measurements students determined. Have students work on their discovery center investigations. Circulate to hear progress and help with any needs that may arise. Evaluate when students will be ready to present. Select a presentation day and announce this deadline. Continue to give students time to work until the presentation day.

➤ Activity Plan 5: Is the Moon Really Made from Green Cheese?

Materials

Pictures of the moon's surface (Seymour Simon's book *The Moon* [New York: Four Winds Press, 1984] and Michael George's book *Moon* [Mankato, MN: Creative Education, 1992] have good pictures. Many of the pictures in the George book are NASA images.)
Large baking pan filled with three inches of sand and a layer of flour on top
Newspapers
Science journals
Scrap materials, anything that could be used to build a lunar rover: cereal boxes, aluminum foil, egg cartons, pipe cleaners, wire, toothpicks, Popsicle sticks, paper plates, cups, bowls, string, rubberbands
Glue
Scissors
"Moon rock" samples: marbles, gravel, pebbles, and small rocks

Engage

Show the pictures of the moon and have students speculate about what causes the light and dark areas of the moon. Ask them what the advisors from the story *Many Moons* would say. (The Lord High Chamberlain might say that the differences were caused by the movement of molten copper; the Royal Wizard would argue for different shades of green (moldy) cheese; the Royal Mathematician would claim different thicknesses of asbestos; Princess Lenore would probably say light and dark areas of gold; and the Court Jester—if we think of the last page of the story—would argue for the light and shadows of the face of the man in the moon.) (*Visual/Spatial Intelligence*)

Elaborate

Ask the students what those areas of the moon are. Refocus question: What makes up the surface of the moon? (*Note:* Students should be able to recall much of this information because of the research chart they completed at the beginning of the study; as each feature of the moon is discussed, have students take notes in their science journals.)

1. Sharp, rough, bare-rock mountains and hills rise from the surface. The Leibnitz Mountains are located near the moon's south pole.

2. Canyons, or rilles as they are called on the moon, wind through its surface. The Hadley Rille is one canyon; it's eighty-four miles long and 1,312 feet deep.

3. Lots of craters mark its surface. Some are small, others are very large; some are shallow, others are very deep. Copernicus is one crater; it is 56 miles wide, with mountains that reach 12,000 feet above the crater floor. Clavius is another crater; it is 146 miles wide. Scientists theorize that the craters have been formed in two ways: by meteorites hitting the moon's surface and by volcanic action.

Spread newspapers on the floor and place the sand and flour pan in the middle of the papers. Have the students stand at the outer edges of the newspaper. To visualize crater formation by meteorite impact, have student volunteers drop some of the moon rock samples (a marble, a piece of gravel, and a rock) into the pan of flour one by one, then carefully lift them out. Change the height from which the moon rocks are released and drop them again into new areas of the pan. Compare and contrast the craters' sizes and shapes.

4. Plains, or maria as they are called on the moon, are the dark areas on the moon. Early astronomers thought they were seas and oceans and that's why they are called maria; *maria* is a Latin word for seas. They were formed billions of years ago when the moon's volcanoes were active. Meteorites crashed to the surface and cracked it, and molten rock bubbled through the cracks, flooding the surface and cooling into wide, flat areas of rock. The maria have interesting names, such as Sea of Tranquility, Sea of Rains, and Ocean of Storms.

5. Analysis of the moon rocks brought back by the *Apollo* astronauts reveals that they are similar to volcanic rock found on Earth and are made of basalt.

6. The surface of the moon is covered with layers of dust, stones, and rock chips because meteorites have smashed the surface rocks into fragments. Scientists call this regolith.

Explore

Ask students how scientists have learned about the surface of the moon. (space probes taking pictures, manned spacecraft landing and exploring on the moon, and telescope observations) During the last three *Apollo* missions, astronauts traveled the surface of the moon in a lunar rover. Wouldn't that be fun!

Have students work with partners and design and build lunar rovers that can pick up moon rock samples (pebbles, marbles, small rocks, or gravel). Use the scrap materials and allow students to contribute supplies from home. (*Interpersonal and Bodily/Kinesthetic Intelligences*)

Connect

Have students demonstrate their lunar rovers' capabilities (pick up moon rock samples) and explain their design processes.

➤ Activity Plan 6: Just for Fun—Fascination with the Moon

Materials

Moon music from Activity Plan 1: Sharing the Story
Drawing paper
Illustrating materials (crayons, multicolored chalk, markers, or colored pencils)
Variety of simple musical instruments (keyboard, horns, drums, rattles)

Engage

Reprise the moon music, then speculate with students why Princess Lenore thought the moon would make her well again.

Elaborate

Introduce the discovery center choices:

1. Just like Princess Lenore, the moon continues to fascinate and intrigue us. There are lots of moon words and phrases listed in the dictionary, and the closing page of the story *Many Moons* illustrates a long-held belief about the moon: that the light and dark spots formed the face of a man who lives in the moon.

2. Share the details of the discovery center choices. Have students select the choices they will pursue and identify how they will proceed. Students should follow these steps:

   • Research word meanings or study pictures of the moon's light and dark areas.

   • Write a rap or a song or prepare a preliminary sketch. Conference with a peer or teacher to discuss possible changes and improvements.

   • Make revisions in the preliminary product.

   • Produce a final product.

   • Rehearse the presentation.

   • Present the product.

Explore

Have students complete the discovery center investigations.

Connect

Have students present their products.

WHAT DO YOU SEE?

From ancient times people have watched the moon in fascination. Some saw a man in the moon, some Hawaiian tales tell of a woman who works in the moon, and the ancient Greeks saw a goddess riding the sky in a silver chariot. Review the list of moon names from colonial American times and from different Native American groups, select one name, and think about how the dark and light spots of the moon could actually portray that name. Plan and make a picture of the moon that illustrates that name. (*Visual/Spatial Intelligence*)

Moon Names

Winter Moon	Wolf Moon
Black Bear Moon	Fish Moon
Crow Moon	Flower Time Moon
Little Frogs Croak Moon	Moon of the Giant Cactus
Spider Web on the Ground at Dawn Moon	Beaver Moon

MOON WORDS GALORE!

The dictionary lists lots of moon words and phrases. Create a song or rap that helps you understand their meanings; add movements to increase understanding. Select five moon words or phrases. (*Musical/Rhythmic Intelligence*)

Moon Words and Phrases

moon ball	moonbeam
mooncalf	mooneye
moonflower	moon gate
moonlet	moonseed
moon shell	moonstone
promise the moon	once in a blue moon
full of the moon	dark of the moon
ask for the moon	

➤Culminating Activity Plan: Lunar Disaster

Materials

Drawing paper
Illustrating materials (markers, crayons, colored pencils)
"Lunar Disaster," *Moonscapes, Windows on Science, Earth Science* 2 (1988) (A laser disc program available from Optical Data Corporation, 30 Technology Dr., Warren, NJ 07059; cost: about $500.)

Engage

Write this date on the board—Sunday, July 20, 1969—and ask students why this date is memorable in space exploration. (Neil Armstrong and Edwin "Buzz" Aldrin landed on the moon, and Neil Armstrong took the first steps, saying as he walked, "That's one small step for man, one giant leap for mankind.")

Elaborate

The *Apollo* moon missions explored the surface of the moon, collected rock samples, and left behind a variety of instruments that would continue to gather information, but since 1972 no astronauts have returned to explore the moon. Scientists may one day return to the moon to set up a lunar space station, but this would take lots of design inventions. People living in the lunar base would need ways to adjust for gravity differences; inventions that provide food, air, and water; and structures that protect them from the temperature extremes, crashing meteorites, and radiation from the sun.

Ask students: What would be the advantages of returning to the moon? Adventure? Mining? Creating new medicines? Experimenting? Observing the universe?

Ask them what the lunar base would look like. Have students work with partners to draw lunar bases. Display the pictures, then introduce the lunar disaster survival activity. (*Interpersonal and Visual/Spatial Intelligences*)

Explore

Divide the class into small groups and have them complete the lunar disaster survival activity. In this activity students must select ten items to help them survive a crash landing on the moon, sixty-five miles from the nearest lunar base. (*Logical/Mathematical and Interpersonal Intelligences*)

Connect

Have student groups share their survival kits and the reasoning behind their decisions.

5 One Fine Day

Written by Nonny Hogrogian
Illustrated by Nonny Hogrogian
New York: Macmillan, 1971

Summary

➤ A greedy fox encounters unexpected consequences when he steals milk from an old woman. She removes his tail and demands the return of her milk. The fox begins a long search for the milk, first asking a cow, who demands some grass; then seeking the grass, but the grass wants water; then finding the water, which requires a jug; then discovering the maiden who holds the jug, which she will not release until she receives a blue bead; then locating a peddler, who has the blue bead but needs an egg; then sighting a hen who's hungry for grain. Finally, in desperation, the fox bargains with a miller for the grain. The fox receives the grain and eventually returns to the old woman with the milk, after which she sews his tail in place.

Award Year

➤ 1972

Art Information

➤ Illustrated using acrylics on gesso panels.

Curriculum Connections

➤ Zoo animals, with emphasis on this science idea: An animal's survival depends on its body structures and behaviors; structures and behaviors help an animal catch food, move around, attract a mate, survive the climate, and protect itself from predators.

➤Activity Plan 1: Sharing the Story

Materials

> Milk (small carton or jar)
> Knife
> Needle and thread
> Grass
> Water
> Jug
> Blue bead
> Egg
> Grain (couscous, wheat germ)
> Caldecott Award poster
> Acrylic pigment (available at art stores)
> Gesso (available at art stores)

Engage

Begin with these brainstorming questions and have students play animal charades to demonstrate their answers. Ask the students: What is the most unusual animal in the zoo you have ever seen? What is the most ordinary animal in the zoo you have ever seen? What animal is most fun to watch? Which animal is most dangerous? (*Bodily/Kinesthetic Intelligence*)

Elaborate

Display these supplies: milk, knife, needle and thread, grass, water, jug, blue bead, egg, grain. Introduce the items to the students and explain that these supplies are part of what happens to the main character of the story, the fox. Ask the students to imagine and tell the story. Begin with this starter, "One fine day a fox traveled through a great forest. When he reached the other side he was very thirsty."

Invite audience responses and use your creative skills, your acting ability, and your familiarity with the story to create a new story based on input from students. Be sure students connect every object. (*Verbal/Linguistic Intelligence*)

Hints: Invite several ideas before selecting the best way to continue with the story. Encourage nonviolent suggestions and a happy ending. For example, one student might suggest that the fox drank the milk and another student might suggest that the fox found a stream and drank the water. The story might continue in this way: "When he reached the other side he was very thirsty; his tongue began to hang from his mouth (do it), his sides began to pant (do it), when suddenly he came upon a clear, cold stream and drank to his heart's content (make slurping noises). He lay exhausted beside the stream, when suddenly . . . " Remove the water from the display and invite additional responses. Continue until all the objects have been removed.

Explore

Read the story. Invite students to compare their version with Nonny Hogrogian's story.

Connect

Ask the students what they notice about the way the story is written. Ask them to evaluate the consequences of the theft. Were they too hard? Were they too easy?

Share the Caldecott Award information:

1. As students examine the cover of the book, ask them what special thing they notice. (gold medal) Ask them what the name of the medal is. (Caldecott Award Medal) Ask them why it has been placed on this book. (Some of the answers might be: The illustrations are special, well done, particularly interesting, exciting, and/or unusual.)

2. Discuss the art techniques used in creating the pictures. Two media contributed to the illustrations seen in this story. Ms. Hogrogian began by coating the canvases with gesso. Gesso is a white pigment that's mixed with whiting, water, and glue. A coating with gesso prepares the canvas and provides the foundation for other paints, because it smoothes the canvas and helps cut down on absorption of the paint. Acrylic paints were also used. Acrylics go on like oil paints but have two advantages: They dry quickly without changing color and they do not darken with time.

3. Ask two student volunteers to search the poster for the year the story won. (Searching the poster helps students become familiar with the many different titles selected for the award.)

➤ Activity Plan 2: Surviving in the Wild

Materials

Books about animals (Be sure each vertebrate group is represented: mammals, reptiles, birds, fish, and amphibians. Schedule a trip to the library and have students select and check out books about animals.)

Six structures and behaviors worksheets for students to record the results of their adaptations research:

- Activity sheet 5.1. Finding Food, Water, and Air
- Activity sheet 5.2. Moving Around
- Activity sheet 5.3. Whew! It's Hot, Brrrr! It's Cold
- Activity sheet 5.4. Getting Away
- Activity sheet 5.5. I Am Special Circle (one per student)
- Activity sheet 5.6. Finding a Mate

cold weather clothing (gloves, coat, hat, scarf)
warm weather clothing (shorts, sandals, T-shirt)

Text continues on page 110.

Finding Food, Water, and Air: What Are the Adaptations?					
Creature	Carnivore	Herbivore	Omnivore	Air	Water

Moving Around: What Are the Adaptations?	
Creature	What Is the Movement and How Does It Happen?

► Activity Sheet 5.2. Moving Around

Whew! It's Hot, Brrr! It's Cold: How Can We Adapt?		
Creatures	Hot Weather Adaptations	Cold Weather Adaptations

▶ Activity Sheet 5.3. Whew! It's Hot, Brrr! It's Cold

Getting Away: How Do We Manage It?	
Creatures	**Escaping the Predators**

➤Activity Sheet 5.4. Getting Away

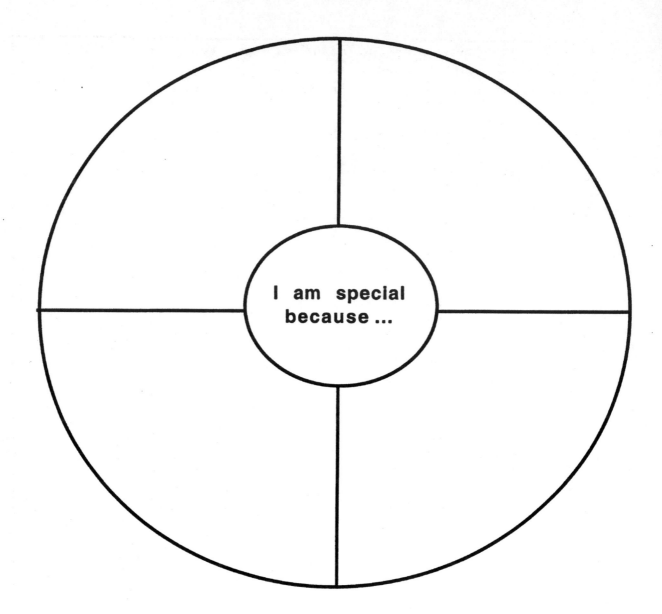

I am special
because ...

➤Activity Sheet 5.5. I Am Special Circle

Finding a Mate: What Are the Adaptations?	
Creature	**How Does It Happen?**

➤Activity Sheet 5.6. Finding a Mate

➤ *Finding Food, Water, and Air*

Engage

Write these words on the board: *food, water, air, ingredients for survival.*

Elaborate

Ask the students: What inventions/structures help human beings meet their food, water, and air needs? (tractors, combines, cooking utensils, grocery stores, knives, forks, spoons, different kinds of ovens, wells, water systems, teeth, digestive system, lungs)

Explore

Ask the students: How do animals get food and water and air? What structures and behaviors help them meet these needs for survival? Have students work with partners and use the animal books to find the ways animals meet their food and water needs and also identify how they meet their oxygen needs. Have students record the information on the food, water, and air chart (see activity sheet 5.1). Students should write the names of their creatures in the first column, select the appropriate column (carnivore, herbivore, or omnivore) to describe the animals' diet, then add information about meeting water and air needs. For example, geese (herbivores) have water-resistant feathers and use their webbed feet and their rounded bills to swim and eat small water plants; penguins use their flippers to propel themselves quickly through the water and their ability to dive to hunt for fish, squids, and krill; and a desert tortoise gets most of its water and food requirements from the plants it eats.

Connect

Review the completed chart to find different ways of meeting food, water, and air needs. (*Verbal/Linguistic and Logical/Mathematical Intelligences*)

➤ *Moving Around*

Engage

Have students stand on tiptoes, stoop, run in place, and skip. (*Bodily/Kinesthetic Intelligence*)

Elaborate

Ask the students: What body structures give us movement? (bones, joints, muscles) What inventions add to our ability to move? (transportation vehicles of all kinds; recreational inventions like roller blades, skis, surf boards)

Explore

Ask the students: What body structures give animals movement? What movements help them survive in their habitats? Have students work with partners and use the animal books to find ways animals move. Record the information on the moving around chart (activity sheet 5.2). For example, the scales on a snake's belly help the animal move by pressing against the ground as the muscles of the snake push its body ahead. Wide foot pads (that work almost like snowshoes) help camels walk easily on loose, shifting sand; the pads spread out and keep the camel from sinking into the sand. The condor has fingerlike feathers at its wing tips; these feathers help the condor soar on warm air currents and steer without flapping its wings.

Connect

Review the completed chart to explore the structures that help animals move. (*Verbal/ Linguistic, Interpersonal, and Logical/Mathematical Intelligences*)

➤ *Climate: Whew! It's Hot, Brrrr! It's Cold*

Engage

Role-play getting dressed for cold weather. "Brrrr! I'm so cold, I need some more clothes." (Don the coat, hat, gloves, and scarf.) "Whew! Now it's too hot!" (Take off the winter clothes and reach for the warm weather clothing.) (*Bodily/Kinesthetic Intelligence*)

Elaborate

Clothing changes are one way human beings survive in different weather. Ask the students to identify other ways we protect ourselves from weather. (umbrellas, cars, air conditioners, heaters, sunscreen)

Explore

Ask the students: How do animals deal with changes in the weather? How do they manage cold weather and hot weather? Have students work with partners, using the animal books to find the adaptations of animals that allow them to deal with hot and cold temperatures. Have the students record the information on the weather chart (activity sheet 5.3). Students should write the names of their creatures in the first column, then describe how the animals adapt to heat and cold. For example, many birds deal with temperature changes by migrating between summer homes and winter homes; they also have undercoats of fluffy down feathers that keep them warm. Polar bears have hair coats that allow them to survive in extremely cold weather; the outer layer of hair is long (which lets water roll off the body) and translucent (which lets sunlight penetrate and warm the black skin underneath). Whales and some species of seals have thick layers of fat, called blubber, just under the skin, which protect them from the cold waters of the North.

Connect

Review the completed chart to find different ways of adapting to temperature changes. (*Verbal/Linguistic, Interpersonal, and Logical/Mathematical Intelligences*)

➤ *Predators: Getting Away*

Engage

Write this word on the board: *Escape!*

Elaborate

Pose this question to students: How do humans know danger is near and escape from it? (acting on information received through our five senses) For example, smells warn of dangers from toxic fumes and fires and sounds warn of dangers from traffic, intruders, weapons, and other animals.

Explore

Ask the students: How do animals protect themselves from dangers? Have students work with partners and use the animal books to explore and find answers to this question. Have them record the information on the getting away chart (activity sheet 5.4). Students should write the names of their creatures in the first column, then describe ways animals escape danger. For example, rabbits have strong hind legs for running quickly and thick fur for protection from the sharp talons of a hawk. Ptarmigans change their protective coloring: In the summer months they grow dark feathers, and in the winter months they shed the dark feathers and grow white feathers that allow them to blend into snowy backgrounds. Turtles have two hinged shells made from hard, bony plates that are joined together; when they are threatened they pull vulnerable parts (head and legs) into the shell and close the flat bottom shell tightly against the domed top shell. When wolves start circling, looking for weak members of the group, musk oxen form a tight circle with their sharp horns pointing out.

Connect

Review the completed chart to find different ways of avoiding dangers from predators. (*Verbal/Linguistic, Interpersonal, and Logical/Mathematical Intelligences*)

➤ *Finding a Mate*

Engage

Have students complete the "I Am Special" circle by drawing or writing ideas in each portion of the circle (activity sheet 5.5). If students are stumped, ideas you could suggest are: I am special because of my name, my hair color, my smile, my friendliness, or my ability to ride my bike, listen to others, share, draw, tell jokes. (*Verbal/Linguistic and Visual/Spatial Intelligences*)

Elaborate

Ask students how they find friends. Refocus question: What makes a person a friend? (Brainstorm a list of qualities and characteristics, then write a class acrostic poem about friends. See figure 5.1 for an example.) Ask students how they let friends know about their special qualities. (*Verbal/ Linguistic Intelligence*)

Friends are ...
Reliable
Important
Exciting
Never mean
Dependable
Sympathetic!

➤ Figure 5.1. Friends Poem

Explore

Ask students: How do animals let each other know about their special qualities? What special abilities do they have that help them find mates? Have students work with partners, using the animal books to explore and find answers to this question. Have them record the information on the finding a mate chart (activity sheet 5.6). Students should write the names of their creatures in the first column, then describe adaptations for attracting mates in the second column. For example, to attract a mate, the male peacock raises his long train of tail feathers, spreads them into a fan, and begins to strut. Male frogs croak to attract females, and elks announce the mating season with loud, bugling calls. The belly of the male stickleback fish turns red when mating season has begun.

Connect

Review the completed chart to see the many ways in which creatures attract each other. (*Verbal/Linguistic, Interpersonal, and Logical/Mathematical Intelligences*)

➤Activity Plan 3: Other Zoo Connections

Materials

Plan a zoo trip and arrange an interview with the zoo dietitian and/or the zoo veterinarian
Science journals

Engage

Review the structures and behaviors posters students completed during Activity Plan 2. Have students use their science journals to write down key words and phrases that will help them to record observations at the zoo (food, water, and air; movement; surviving the weather; escaping from predators; finding a mate).

Elaborate

Take the zoo trip and remind students to use their science journals to observe and record the structures and behaviors they see that help animals survive. Interview the zoo dietitian or the zoo veterinarian.

Explore

Discuss and share experiences from the zoo trip. Offer students the following two extension choices.

LIVING AT THE ZOO

Increasingly, zoo animals live in habitats that closely resemble their homes in the wild. Design a new zoo habitat and create a diorama that shows your plan. Think about these questions: What animals will live together in the habitat? How will human visitors view the habitat? How will zoo caretakers have access to the habitat? (*Bodily/Kinesthetic Intelligence*)

ZOO CARTOONS

If animals could talk, they might say some funny things. Imagine a conversation between two animals at the zoo. Then draw the animals and create conversation balloons that show what they are discussing. (*Visual/Spatial Intelligence*)

Connect

Display the finished products. Take a tour and have each student speak briefly about his or her creation.

➤ Activity Plan 4: Creating a New Story

Materials

Chart paper listing components of the story
Marker
Large sheets of white construction paper
Illustrating materials (crayons, markers, paints, or colored pencils)

Engage

Ask the students how *One Fine Day* would change if the story took place at the zoo. Use wait time to give students opportunities to think about changes this would require in the story.

Elaborate

Explore the possibilities with students by first looking at the story components of *One Fine Day*. Create a chart like the one below, then slowly review the chart to remind students of the story structure they are changing.

One Fine Day	*Our new story*
forest	zoo
woman gathering wood	
fox	
steals the milk	
cuts off his tail	
begs for his tail	
gives a command	
goes to the cow and begs	
goes to the grass and begs	
goes to the water and begs	
goes to the girl and begs	
goes to the peddler and begs	
goes to the chicken and begs	
goes to the miller and begs	
gets the grain	
gets the egg	
gets the blue bead	
gets the jug	
gets the water	
gets the grass	
gets the milk	
gets back his tail	

Explore

Ask the students: How can we place our story in the zoo? What animals, places, people will we choose? Help the students use the chart to construct substitute ideas for the story. (*Logical/ Mathematical Intelligence*)

In the example in figure 5.2 the students identified a wolf and her two children as the main characters of the story; the problem became the egg the wolf stole (and ate) from the ostrich. The teacher responded with this question: What animals in the zoo also lay eggs? The students selected an emu. Then the question became: What payment would the emu demand? Two students suggested researching the diet of the emu; a quick look at the encyclopedia with the teacher's help resulted in the suggestion of corn. That idea produced this question: What would be a source of corn at the zoo? Answer: The zookeeper. The teacher asked the students the following questions to build the new story:

What might the zookeeper enjoy? (butterflies)

What adjective (describing word) would you say about the zookeeper? (wonderful, kind, thoughtful, caring)

What might the butterflies need? (nectar, flowers)

What would be a source of flowers or who cares for the flowers? (greenhouse keeper)

What might the greenhouse keeper demand? (birds, parrots, toucans)

What would the birds require? (peanuts)

Where will the wolf find peanuts? (from the elephants)

What will the elephants ask of the wolf? (apples, other fruit)

Who eats apples and other fruit? (monkeys)

What are characteristics of monkeys? (chatter, make noise)

The monkeys became the substitutes for the miller and gave the wolf what she needed, and the story reversed.

Connect

Have students work in partnership to illustrate the new tale, add a title, and bind the pages into a book. (*Visual/Spatial Intelligence*)

Hints: After the brainstorming session the teacher can use the chart and a word processing program to create text for a class book. Creation of the text can be a flexible activity, depending on the abilities and attention of the students. Sometimes the creation of the substitute ideas for the chart is challenging enough; sometimes the children enjoy creating the actual text. This would happen in another session and is greatly facilitated by gathering students in front of the computer. In the example from the first-grade class (see figure 5.2), the students brainstormed the chart, but the teacher created the actual text based on the ideas of the chart.

Print the text, cut it into decorative strips, and paper-clip the strips to the construction paper pages. The student partnerships should then select the pages they wish to illustrate. Have students plan their illustrations and the placement of the text (rough draft) on separate sheets of paper, then use the construction paper to make final drawings. Because the text has not yet been pasted to the picture, making mistakes or needing to start over is not a problem. Have students paste the text on when the drawings are finished.

Title Page: <u>A Bad Day for the Wolf at the Zoo</u>

Created by:

Dedication Page: Dedicated to our teacher and our library, and to our zoo friends

Page 1: One bad day a wolf and her two children wandered through the zoo. When they reached the ostrich pen, they were very hungry.

Page 2: The mother wolf saw an egg that the ostrich had laid. Before the ostrich noticed the wolf and her two children, she and her children had gobbled the egg.

Page 3: The ostrich became so angry that she grabbed the two children and would not let them go. The wolf began to cry, "Please return my two children because I will miss them so." "Return my egg," she said, "and I will return your two children."

Page 4: The wolf dried her tears and went to find an emu. "Dear emu," she begged, "please give me an egg so I can give it to the ostrich and she will return my two children." The emu replied, "I'll give you an egg if you bring me some corn."

Page 5: The wolf ran to the zookeeper, "Oh wonderful zookeeper, give me an ear of corn. I'll take it to the emu and she will give me an egg. Then I'll take the egg to the ostrich so she will return my two children." The zookeeper called back, "Bring me some butterflies."

Page 6: The wolf ran to the butterfly house and begged them to follow her to the zookeeper. The butterflies answered, "Bring us a bouquet of pretty flowers."

Page 7: The wolf found the greenhouse keeper. "Please kind sir," she said, "please give me a bouquet of pretty flowers, so I can take them to the butterflies, so they will follow me to the zookeeper, so I can get an ear of corn to take to the emu, so the emu will give me an egg to give to the ostrich, so the ostrich will return my two children." The greenhouse keeper smiled, "If you find a flock of beautiful birds to sing in my greenhouse," he said, "I will give you a bouquet of pretty flowers."

➤ Figure 5.2. Sample Alternate Tale

Page 8: So the wolf found the aviary, and spoke to the toucans, "There is a greenhouse keeper down the road, and if you come to the greenhouse and sing for him, he will be pleased with you and pleased with me. Then he will give me a bouquet of pretty flowers, so I can take them to the butterflies, so they will follow me to the zookeeper, so I can get an ear of corn to take to the emu, so the emu will give me an egg to give to the ostrich, so the ostrich will return my two children." But the toucans were not taken in by the promise of a pretty smile or the cleverness of the wolf and replied, "Pay us some peanuts and we will sing for the greenhouse keeper."

Page 9: The wolf went off and found the elephants. "Elephants, dear elephants, please give me some peanuts to give to the toucans so they will sing for the greenhouse keeper, so he will give me a bouquet of pretty flowers, so I can take them to the butterflies, so they will follow me to the zookeeper, so I can get an ear of corn to take to the emu, so the emu will give me an egg to give to the ostrich, so the ostrich will return my two children." The elephants trumpeted, "We'll trade you some peanuts for some crunchy apples and a ripe banana."

Page 10: The wolf was getting desperate! When she found the monkeys she began to cry. "Oh kind monkeys, please give me some crunchy apples and a ripe banana. I have to trade them for some peanuts to give to the toucans so they will sing for the greenhouse keeper, so he will give me a bouquet of pretty flowers, so I can take them to the butterflies, so they will follow me to the zookeeper, so I can get an ear of corn to take to the emu, so the emu will give me an egg to give to the ostrich, so the ostrich will return my two children."

Page 11: The monkeys were in a good mood and chattering happily and felt sorry for the wolf. They gave her the fruit to give to the elephants to trade for the peanuts to give to the toucans.

Page 12: So they will sing for the greenhouse keeper, so he will give a bouquet of pretty flowers, to take to the butterflies, so they will go to the zookeeper.

Page 13: So she can get an ear of corn to take to the emu, so the emu will give an egg to give to the ostrich, so the ostrich will return the two children.

Page 14: The wolf returned to the ostrich and gave him the egg. Then she willingly returned the two children, and off ran the wolf and her two children to the other side of the zoo.

➤ Figure 5.2. Sample Alternate Tale (*cont.*)

6　The Snowy Day

Written by Ezra Jack Keats
Illustrated by Ezra Jack Keats
New York: The Viking Press, 1962

Summary

➤ Peter awakens to a snow-covered neighborhood and spends a wonderful day adventuring in the snow. He crunches in the snow with his toes pointing straight ahead, then pointing sideways; he finds a stick and makes a new track, then uses the stick to smack a snow-covered tree; he builds a smiling snowman and carves snow angels; he pretends to be a mountain climber, then slides down the hill; finally he packs a handful of snow, tucking it securely in the pocket of his coat. He tells his mother all about his adventures as he prepares for bed, hoping the snow will remain for another adventurous day.

Award Year

➤ 1963

Art Information

➤ Illustrated using collage.

Curriculum Connections

➤ Matter, with emphasis on this science idea: Matter takes up space and has weight; there are three states of matter—solids, liquids, and gases.

➤Activity Plan 1: Sharing the Story

Materials

Prefolded paper in preparation for making snowflakes:
- eight-pointed snowflake: Fold a square piece of paper diagonally in half, fold in half again, and again.
- six-pointed snowflake: Fold a square piece of paper in half, fold it in half again, and again.

Scissors
Activity sheet 6.1, Snowman Shape (one per student)
Miscellaneous materials: pipe cleaners, felt/other materials, buttons, beads, lace, yarn, fake fur, toothpicks, cotton, construction paper, etc.
Caldecott Award poster
Tissue paper (white and one or two other colors)
Small cup of water
Paintbrush
Wallpaper sample
Cotton balls or batting (a small piece)
Old toothbrush and small piece of screen
Black and dark green construction paper, small sheets

Engage

Using the pre-folded paper, ask for shape suggestions from the students, begin to make cuts in the paper, and design the snowflake (don't tell them what you are making). Slowly unfold the snowflake. Repeat the process with a second paper. (*Visual/Spatial Intelligence*)

Ask the students: Snow represents what state of matter? (solid) How would you define a solid? (At this point, you are just inviting speculation and thinking; some answers might be: takes up space, has size, can be touched, has a shape, stays the same.) What are the other states of matter? (liquids and gases) How are they different from a solid? (Again, this is a thinking question; possible answers might be: Liquids run and don't hold their shapes, gases can't be seen.)

Elaborate

Introduce the story and ask students to compare Peter's experiences with their own favorite snow memories.

Explore

Have students share favorite snow memories.

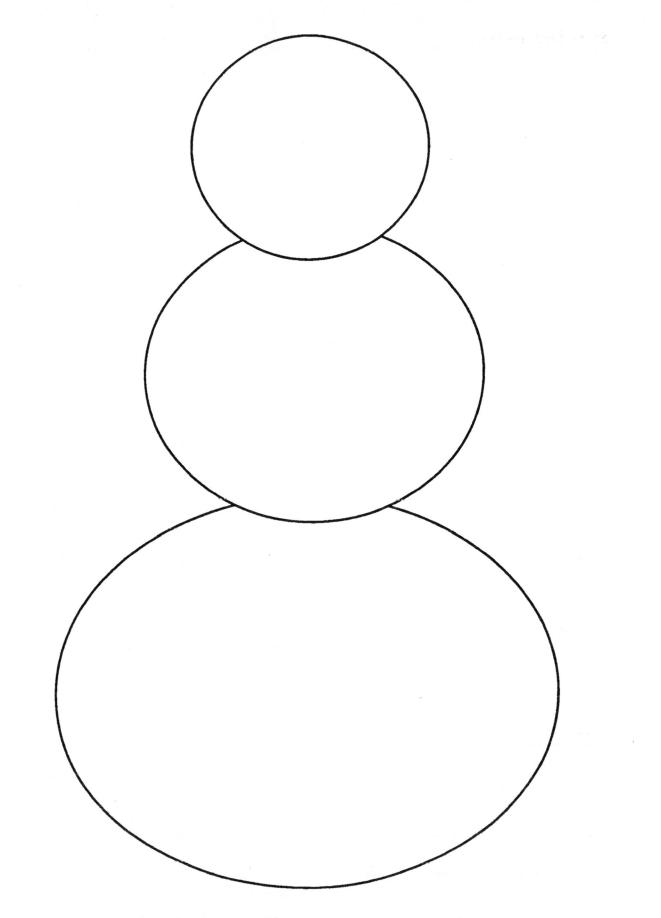

➤Activity Sheet 6.1. Snowman Shape

Share the Caldecott Award information:

1. As students examine the cover of the book, ask them what special thing they notice. (gold medal) Ask them the name of the medal. (Caldecott Award Medal) Ask them why it has been placed on this book. (Some of the answers may be: The illustrations are special, well done, particularly interesting, exciting, and/or unusual.)

2. Discuss collage, the illustrating technique used in this story. Collage is an art technique in which the artist gathers many materials and uses them to create the pictures we see.

   Show students the materials you have gathered (tissue paper, wallpaper sample, cotton balls, the toothbrush and a small piece of screen, and the black/green construction paper) and explore understanding of collage.

   > Tissue paper: Show students the title page and the snow and backgrounds on pages 8–15 of the story. Keats layered tissue paper to create these effects. (Layer the tissue paper and use the paintbrush dipped in water to blend the colors.) Let students examine the papers to note how the colors underneath merge with the white.

   > Wallpaper sample: Show students pages 6–7, 25, and 28–30 and note the wallpaper samples used to create Peter's pajamas, the wall covering of his room, and his mother's dress.

   > Cotton balls: Pull the cotton into thin, wispy strands, then show students the clouds on pages 22 and 23.

   > Toothbrush/screen: Rub the toothbrush against the screen and ask students to speculate about the effect this would create if the toothbrush had been dipped in black paint. (Spatter paint droplets would result.) Look at pages 28 and 29 for illustrations of this effect.

   > Black/green construction paper: Tell the students that cutting these to the required shapes could have created Peter's bed frame (pages 6–7), the fence (pages 8–9), the stoplight (page 11), and the stool (page 25).

3. Ask two student volunteers to search the Caldecott Award poster for the year this story won. (Searching the poster helps students become familiar with the many different titles selected for the award.)

Connect

Have students use the snowman shapes (activity sheet 6.1) and the collage technique (using the gathered miscellaneous materials) to create snow people. Suggestions include Michael Jordan (basketball player), Neil Armstrong (astronaut), Winnie the Pooh (bear), Bigfoot (monster), George Washington (president), Miss Wise Owl, Mr. Porcupine, Jimmy Cottontail (rabbit), Wilbur (pig), Sherlock Holmes (detective), Mr. Popper's penguin, and Puss in Boots (cat). Share and display the finished products. (*Visual/Spatial Intelligence*)

➤ Activity Plan 2: States of Matter

Materials

Glass of water and something quick to eat (for the teacher)
Chart for exploring solid matter; enlarge it or use masking tape to outline the chart
  on the floor (see figure 6.1)
Science journals
Large shallow container of water
Measurement chart (see figure 6.2)
Two or three measuring cups
Paper towels
Two-liter bottle filled with water
Small container of perfume or aftershave lotion

Team 1	Team 2	Team 3	Team 4	Team 5
This chair is a solid, because it has a certain shape; it's made out of wood, which doesn't change shape when we sit on it. It also has size. The seat measures 12 inches by 14 inches, the legs are 20 inches tall and the back is 20 inches tall.				

➤ Figure 6.1. Examples of Solids

Student	Amount of Water

➤ Figure 6.2. Measurement Chart

Engage

Ask students to breathe deeply several times, then ask them: What form of matter are you breathing? (gas, because they are breathing air) Drink a glass of water and eat a piece of food. Ask the students what forms of matter these are. (Liquid, because you drank water; solid, because you ate food, a solid substance.)

Elaborate

Have students work with partners to find examples of solids and write in their own words why the objects they chose are solids. Use the chart in figure 6.1 to display the examples and the explanations of why each object is a solid. Discuss the chart display and draw conclusions about the characteristics of solid matter. (Solid matter has shape and takes up space.) Have students record this information in their science journals. (*Logical/Mathematical and Interpersonal Intelligences*)

Explore

Investigate liquid matter. Begin with the shallow pan of water and ask students to use one hand to scoop some water. Measure the amount of water scooped by each student and record the amounts on the chart (see figure 6.2).

Contrast this experience with the solid matter examples and draw conclusions about the characteristics of liquid matter: Ask students what the greatest difference was between this experience (trying to scoop water) and picking up solid matter. (Some responses might be: Liquids don't stay put very well, we had trouble holding and picking up the water, it would be easier if we had some kind of container, the water spread out in my hand and began to drip.) Discuss these conclusions with students: Liquid matter is any kind of matter that flows; liquid matter takes the shape of the container in which it is stored. Have students record this information in their journals, then work with partners to brainstorm examples of liquid matter. (milk, juices, oil, syrup, paint, ink, vinegar, etc.)

Have students breathe deeply again and point out that the air we breathe is a gas. Shake the bottle of water and show the air bubbles that are created. The air bubbles in the bottle did not retain their shape. Ask students what they conclude from this example. (Gas is matter that has no shape or size of its own.)

Have a student volunteer stand in the back or front of the classroom with the closed container of perfume or aftershave lotion. Open the container and gently wave it in the air to release the smell. How quickly does the smell reach the back of the classroom (or the front if the student is standing at the back)? Ask students what they conclude from this example. (Gas spreads out quickly and can fill any size container, like the room. The same amount of gas can fill a small jar, like the perfume container, or the room.) Have students record this information in their journals, then work with partners to brainstorm other examples of gaseous substances. (neon in neon signs, helium in balloons, propane in outdoor grills, freon in air conditioners, etc.)

Connect

Create a Venn diagram that compares the three states of matter and have students record the information in their journals. (See figure 6.3.)

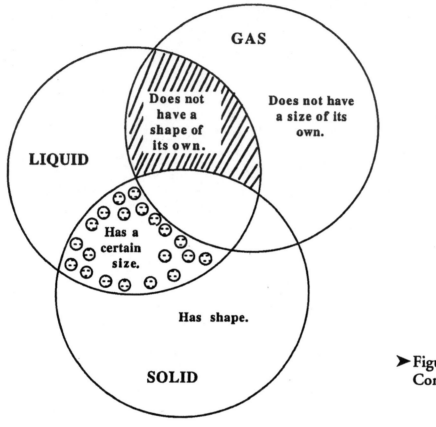

➤Figure 6.3. Venn Diagram: Comparing States of Matter

➤Activity Plan 3: Exploring Changes in Matter

Materials

Science journals
Activity sheet 6.2, States of Matter Investigation Sheet (one per partnership)
Activity sheet 6.3, Melting Times Chart
Baggies
Ice cubes (one per partnership)
Various materials for making things melt quickly (wool scarf, hot water bottle, towel, running water source, etc.)
Stopwatch

Names_____

States of Matter

1. What are some ways to melt ice cubes quickly? _____

_____

2. State a hypothesis: Choose the idea that you think will melt the ice cube in the shortest time. Be sure to explain why.

_____

_____

_____

_____

3. Get your ice cube in a baggie, wait for the teacher's starting signal, then try your idea.

4. How long does it take for the ice cube to melt? _____

5. Compare your results with other partnerships.

	Names	Melting Time
Partnership #1:		
Partnership #2		
Partnership #3:		
Partnership #4:		

6. What conclusions can you draw? _____

_____

_____

➤ Activity Sheet 6.2. States of Matter Investigation Sheet

Teams	Melting Times	Melting Ideas
Partnership #1		
Partnership #2		
Partnership #3		
Partnership #4		
Partnership #5		
Partnership #6		
Partnership #7		
Partnership #8		
Partnership #9		
Partnership #10		

▶ Activity Sheet 6.3. Melting Times Chart

Engage

Peter was disappointed when the snowball melted. Ask the students how he could have prevented this. Have students work with partners to brainstorm lists of ideas in their science journals, then share some of the ideas. (freezer, dry ice, ice chest, bowl surrounded by ice cubes)

Elaborate

From the story we know that the snowball changed from solid matter to liquid matter when it melted in the warm air of the house. Peter wanted to save his snowball, but there are many situations in which snow or ice can be problems (car windshields covered in snow and ice, icy bridges), and people need quick ways to melt or remove it. Ask students to identify other problems with snow and ice.

Have students work in partnerships to investigate ways to make ice cubes melt quickly. Use the changing states of matter investigation sheet (see activity sheet 6.2). (*Logical/Mathematical and Interpersonal Intelligences*)

Explore

Discuss the investigation. Record melting times on the chart (activity sheet 6.3) for all partnerships. Ask the students: What idea produced the shortest melting time? Why was this idea effective? What other ideas produced short melting times? (Hot water and sunlight focused through a magnifying glass were two successful examples used by two student partnerships.)

Connect

Have students make generalizations from the investigation. (Some responses might be: Matter can change states; heat can cause some kinds of solid matter to melt.)

➤ Culminating Activity Plan: Just for Fun, Making Ice Cream

Materials

Small bowls
Spoons
Ice cream freezer (ask a student or another teacher to lend one)
Ice
Salt
Wire whip or electric mixer (for blending the vanilla mixture)

Ingredients for vanilla ice cream (makes one gallon):
- 4 eggs
- 2½ cups of sugar
- 7 cups of milk
- 2 cups of whipping cream
- 2½ tablespoons of vanilla
- ½ teaspoon of salt

Mix the eggs and sugar together until they are thick and light in color. Mix in the rest of the ingredients (be sure everything is smooth and well blended) and pour the mixture into the freezer container. Follow the directions for using the ice cream freezer. Serve when frozen and, while students are eating, discuss what has happened. (The mixture in the freezer container slowly transferred [lost] its warmth to the surrounding ice and salt mixture. The mixture in the freezer container lost so much of its heat that it froze and the ice melted. The mixture changed from liquid matter to solid matter.)

7 Song and Dance Man

Written by Karen Ackerman
Illustrated by Stephen Gammell
New York: Alfred A. Knopf, 1988

Summary

➤ Grandpa relives his vaudeville days as a song and dance man as he shares the contents of his "leather-trimmed trunk" with his grandchildren. While Grandma prepares supper in the kitchen, Grandpa and the grandchildren trek to the attic to return to the good old days. Grandpa opens the trunk and dresses for his show, which includes dancing, singing, jokes, and magic; the grandchildren are entranced and clap enthusiastically at the close of the last dance. Grandpa repacks the trunk and gives the grandchildren hugs as he reminds them he "wouldn't trade a million good old days for the days he spends with them."

Award Year

➤ 1989

Art Information

➤ Illustrated using line drawings in colored pencil.

Curriculum Connections

➤ Human body, with emphasis on this science idea: The systems of the human body work together to give us energy from foods we eat and the air we breathe; to provide protection from injury, to supply movement, coordination, and control; and to help us reproduce.

➤Activity Plan 1: Sharing the Story

Materials

A large open area
Caldecott Award poster
Colored pencils

Engage

Gather in a large circle and have students slowly wake up the muscles of the body. (*Bodily/ Kinesthetic Intelligence*)

Figure 7.1 lists some suggested movements.

1. Start with toes: Raise big toes several times, wiggle the rest of the toes, arch one foot then the other, repeat several times, lift up on tiptoes several times.

2. Pretend to be standing on cotton clouds and jump lightly ten times.

3. Stand firmly on one leg and slowly swing the other leg in a slowly widening arc (front, back, front, back). Repeat with the other leg.

4. Stand with knees slightly bent, bend over and let arms hang loosely; gently shake and wiggle arms; intertwine fingers, palms facing downward and slowly straighten body; continue to slowly raise arms (fingers intertwined) until they are well above the head; stretch (with feet flat) and breathe deeply; relax; stretch (with feet flat) and breathe deeply again; breathe deeply and slowly stretch up on tiptoes, hold, then slowly relax. Slowly return arms to sides.

5. Pretend to look for someone behind you. Inhale and slowly turn the head to one side (no one there); breathe out and slowly return head to the front. Repeat looking over the other shoulder. Repeat twice more.

6. Pretend to shoot an arrow into the sky. Stand with feet shoulder-width apart; pretend to grasp a bow in one hand. Fit an imaginary arrow to the bow and aim and release it toward the sky.

➤Figure 7.1. Muscle Movements

Elaborate

Now that the muscles of the body are awake, have students work with partners and create movements that mirror and mix together and represent ideas/objects/activities. (*Interpersonal and Bodily/Kinesthetic Intelligences*)

Explore

Introduce the story by asking: What is a song and dance man? How are muscles important to his job? As students listen and watch, encourage them to pay special attention to the sounds of the story. Share the story.

Connect

Tell the students the story makes you smile, then ask them: What do you think Grandpa means at the end when he smiles at the children as they leave the attic and says that he wouldn't trade a million good old days for the days he spends with his grandchildren?

Tell the students the story also makes you eager to get up and move again. Ask them what sounds they imagine. (the soft, slippery sounds of Grandpa's tap shoes like rain on a tin roof, the silvery tap of two feet, the sounds like a woodpecker tapping on a tree, a canyon echo as Grandpa sings, the tapping of the finale with sounds that seem too many for only two feet) Explore some of Grandpa's dance movements or ask students who are taking dance classes to teach the class some movements.

Share the Caldecott Award information:

1. As students examine the cover of the book, ask them what special thing they notice. (gold medal) Ask them what the name of the medal is. (Caldecott Award Medal) Ask them why it has been placed on this book. (Some responses might be: The illustrations are special, well done, particularly interesting, exciting, and/or unusual.)

2. Discuss the art techniques used in creating the pictures. Colored pencil was the medium for the illustrations. (Browse the illustrations to reinforce this; for example, on page 1 the pencil lines are particularly noticeable in Grandpa's pants and the chair; on the next page, in the floor and the wall; and on the page illustrating arrival in the attic, the clothes, the wall, and the floor.)

3. Ask two student volunteers to search the poster for the year the story won. (Searching the poster helps students become familiar with the many different titles selected for the award.)

➤Activity Plan 2: The Human Body Machine

Materials

Drawing paper
Illustrating materials (crayons, markers, colored pencils)
Scissors
Old magazines
Bulletin board or display space (Students will illustrate examples of the systems of the human body at work.)
Staples or thumbtacks

Engage

Use the board to draw the web in figure 7.2. This will help students visualize the systems and parts of the body in terms of the basic functions they serve. (*Verbal/Linguistic Intelligence*)

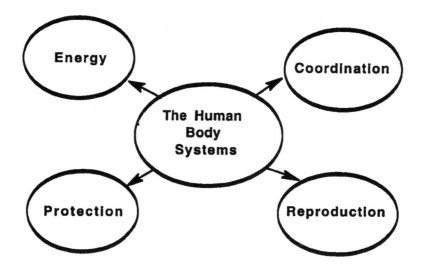

➤Figure 7.2. Human Body Systems

Add information to the web as students respond to these questions (see figure 7.3):

1. What are sources of energy for the body? Refocus question: What parts of the body provide food, water, and air to the body? (stomach, intestines, mouth, the digestive system; lungs, the breathing system; blood, heart, veins, the circulatory system.)

2. What protects the body? Refocus question: What keeps our insides safe? (skin, hair, nails, the covering system; the bones, the skeletal or supporting system; kidneys, bladder, the waste disposal system)

3. What gives the body coordination and movement? Refocus question: What helps us think and how do we control what we do and say? (muscles, the muscular system; brain, nerves, the nervous system)

4. Reproduction is controlled by the reproductive system.

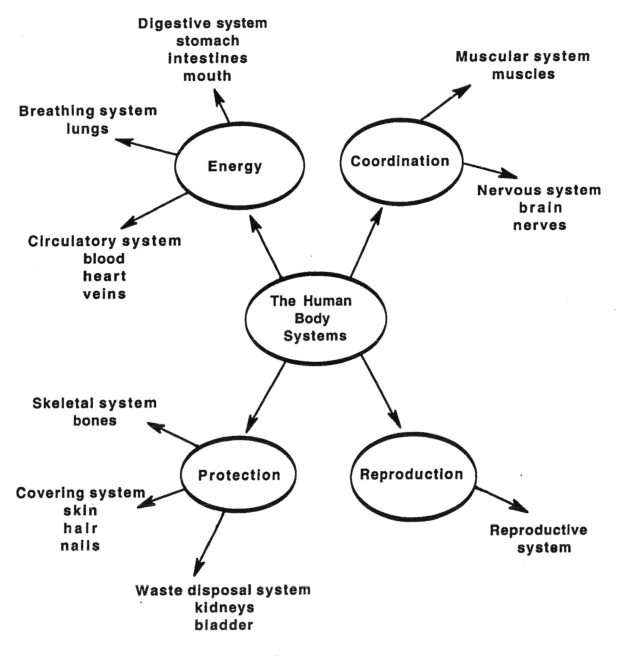

➤Figure 7.3. Human Body Systems Web

Elaborate

Grandpa's performance in the attic shows a picture of the muscular system at work. Ask the students: What activity would show the digestive system at work? (a person eating) What activity would show the nervous system at work? (a person studying or reading) What activity would show the breathing system at work? (a person running) If you smile or frown, which system is working? (muscular) When you see an egg, like a chicken's egg, what system of the body does that represent? (reproductive) When you see a toilet bowl, what system will be helped by this tool? (waste disposal system)

Use the board to list the systems of the body, then list an idea or question for each system that will help students find or draw pictures of activities showing the systems at work (see figure 7.4).

The Systems of the Body at Work	
Covering System	Our skin, hair, and nails: How do they help us?
Skeletal System	Our bones: How do they protect us? What would happen if I didn't have bones?
Muscular System	Our muscles: Remember, they help everything move!
Circulatory System	Our heart and blood: How do they help us?
Breathing System	Think about coughing, sneezing, hiccupping, crying, and laughing.
Digestive System	What are you eating and drinking?
Waste Disposal System	Phew! It's hot outside today! How do we get rid of what we don't need?
Nervous System	How do the five senses help us?
Reproductive System	What pictures represent new life?

➤ Figure 7.4. Systems of the Body at Work

Explore

Have students draw pictures and/or cut pictures from magazines to show the systems of the body at work. (*Visual/Spatial Intelligence*)

Connect

Create a bulletin board display as students share their products and explain how their pictures illustrate the systems at work.

➤Activity Plan 3: Energy for the Body—The Ingredients

Materials

Small cups of water, one per student
Fruit slivers or crackers or bread wedges or some other simple food item that is easy to serve (choose one item)
Science journals
Slips of paper listing the major organs of the digestive and respiratory systems (Place them in two containers, respiratory organs in one, digestive organs in the other; see figure 7.5.)
Two large sheets of butcher paper, long enough so two body outlines can be traced and cut out (Have a student lie lengthwise on the paper and another student trace the outline of the body.)
Transparency of figure 7.6 (states the required steps for the research on the digestive and breathing systems)

Engage

Ask the students: What gives us the energy to run (have students run in place), stretch (have students reach for the floor, then reach high above them), walk (have students follow you to an open space), rest (have students sit or lounge on the floor), jump up (have students stand and return to tables or desks), and read (have students begin reading)? Answers may include food, water, vitamins, minerals, air, and blood. (*Bodily/Kinesthetic Intelligence*)

Elaborate

Serve and consume the food and water. Ask students how that food and water become energy for the body. Invite speculation. Take several deep breaths. Invite students to speculate on what happens to the air we breathe.

Text continues on page 142.

Mouth

Food pipe (Esophagus)

Stomach

Small intestine

Large intestine

Nose

Windpipe

Bronchial tubes

Lungs

➤ Figure 7.5. Organs of the Digestive and Respiratory Systems

Here are the Assignments!	
Digestive System	Breathing System
1. Trace and cut an outline of the human body.	1. Trace and cut an outline of the human body.
2. Choose assignments and work with partners to research the parts of the system to find out how they work and the jobs they do.	2. Choose assignments and work with partners to research the parts of the system to find out how they work and the jobs they do.
3. Construct models of the parts to show how they work.	3. Construct models of the parts to show how they work.
4. Draw and cut out the parts of the digestive system, then place them in the human body outline.	4. Draw and cut out the parts of the breathing system, then place them in the human body outline.
5. Report to the class. •Report on each part of the system and tell how it works and what it does. •Report on the system as a whole. •Answer questions that the class may have.	5. Report to the class. •Report on each part of the system and tell how it works and what it does. •Report on the system as a whole. •Answer questions that the class may have.

➤ Figure 7.6. Research Assignments

Explore

The system of the body that helps food become energy is the digestive system, and the system of the body that helps the body use air is the breathing or respiratory system. Have half of the students find out about the digestive system and half explore the work of the breathing system. Use the transparency of figure 7.6 to review the jobs, then choose assignments by drawing research topic slips from the containers. Have student partnerships or groups begin working on their research assignments. Remind them to use their science journals to record information and sketches. Some groups will finish more quickly than others, so they can trace and cut out the body outlines and draw, cut, and place the system parts in the bodies. Be sure to remind them of basic safety rules for using scissors. Circulate to help partnerships develop clear understandings of how the organs work and the jobs they perform. (*Verbal/Linguistic, Bodily/Kinesthetic, Visual/Spatial, and Interpersonal Intelligences*)

Connect

Have student groups present the systems and answer any questions from the class. To summarize, return to the question posed at the beginning of the lesson: How do food, water, and air become sources of energy for the body? Some responses may be: The small intestine finishes the job of digestion and provides nutrients to the blood; the tiny air sacs in the lungs take carbon dioxide out and put oxygen into the bloodstream, where the oxygen "hitches a ride" on the red blood cells; the delivery system for the air and nutrients is the blood.

➤ Activity Plan 4: Energy for the Body—Delivery

Materials

Small rubber balls that can be squeezed, or tennis balls (one per student)
Heart Highway Model (Enlarge figure 7.7 on a large sheet of butcher paper so it can be laid on the floor and students can gather around it to participate in the demonstration of how the heart works.)
Toy dump truck
Small manipulatives (one color for oxygen, a second color for carbon dioxide, and a third color for nutrients)
Science journals

Engage

Have students make fists, then relax them; repeat several times. The heart works in a similar way: It tightens and pushes blood out of the heart (make a fist); it relaxes and blood comes into the heart (relax the fist). (*Bodily/Kinesthetic Intelligence*)

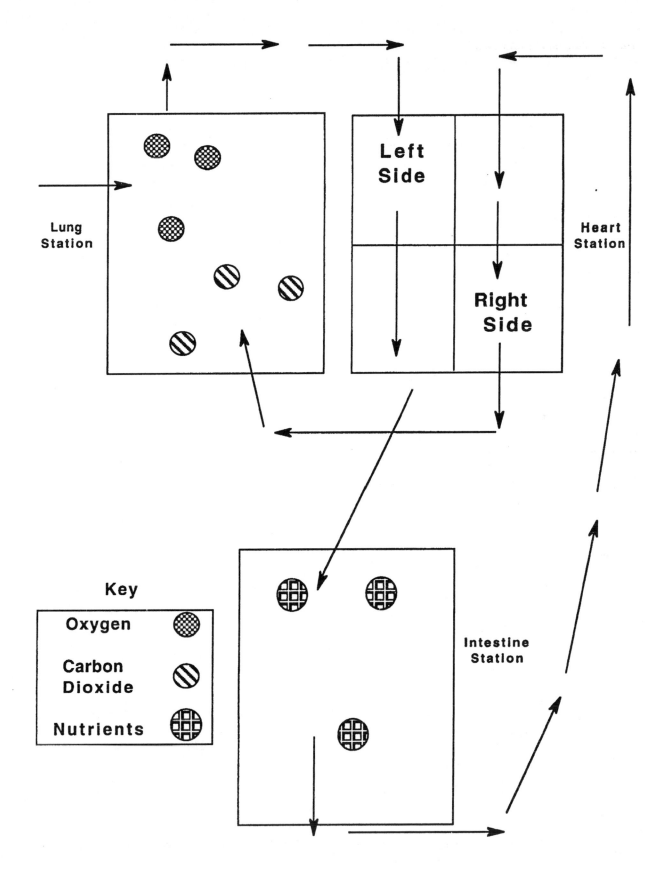

➤ Figure 7.7. Heart Highway Model

Elaborate

Distribute the balls and have students explore the pumping of the heart. Have them give a hard squeeze to the ball; this is the tightening force that happens in the heart and it's needed to pump the blood. It happens over and over and we don't even think about it. The heart in an adult beats about seventy times per minute. Have students try to rhythmically squeeze the ball seventy times in one minute. Ask them to describe what happens. (hands cramp, it's hard work) (*Bodily/Kinesthetic Intelligence*)

The heart is part of the delivery system of the body. Ask students what else is needed to make deliveries of air and nutrients happen. (veins, blood)

Explore

Ask students to identify, from their work with the digestive and breathing systems, the delivery job of the circulatory system. (to spread oxygen and nutrients throughout our body and to gather up the carbon dioxide and return it to the lungs) Ask them how the circulatory system works.

Use the enlarged model of figure 7.7, the manipulatives, the dump truck, and the analogy of a highway system to help explain how the system works. Explain as you demonstrate (*Bodily/Kinesthetic Intelligence*):

1. We learned that one job of the lungs is to bring oxygen to the body, so we will spread the oxygen particles (four to six manipulatives) in the lung station.

2. We also learned that the small intestine finishes the digestive process and makes nutrients available for the body, so we will spread these particles in the intestine station.

3. We also learned that another job of the lungs is to get rid of carbon dioxide from the body, so we will spread the carbon dioxide particles all around the system, and we'll even put some carbon dioxide particles in each room of the heart station and in the lung and intestine stations.

4. Our dump truck is currently parked in the lung station picking up oxygen for delivery (place oxygen manipulatives in the bed of the truck) and it's ready to start traveling. We will move from the lung station to the upper left door in the heart station and deliver oxygen and pick up carbon dioxide, then when the door (valve of the heart) opens we will move to the next room in the heart station and do the same thing: deliver oxygen and pick up carbon dioxide.

5. Now we are ready to move through the rest of our system, delivering oxygen and retrieving carbon dioxide as we go. We'll take a winding path as we move toward the intestine station because every part of our road system requires oxygen and needs to get rid of carbon dioxide. (Exchange oxygen manipulatives for carbon dioxide manipulatives.)

6. As we enter the intestine station, we are ready for some food and we will pick up nutrients, but we will also deliver some oxygen, and let's not forget that carbon dioxide waste.

7. Now we have some extra stuff to deliver along with our oxygen and carbon dioxide exchange. We will continue on our journey and drop some nutrients along the way along with our oxygen. Cells use these nutrients and oxygen to make energy.

8. We have quite a load of carbon dioxide, so let's head back to the heart station and get ready to dump it. We will enter the upper right door, then when the door to this room (lower right, like the lower right valve of the heart) opens, we'll move here; we are almost there. Now for the journey back to the lungs; we're here and ready to dump the carbon dioxide. Oh good, the lungs have carried it away. (Dump the carbon dioxide and sweep it away with your hand, and as your hand returns to the station, drop the reserved pile of oxygen manipulatives in the lung station.)

9. We're ready to begin again with a new delivery. I see the lungs have done their work and brought a new supply of oxygen for delivery. I also see we still have some food to deliver; with this food and oxygen the cells of the lungs will make energy and the lungs will use that energy to continue their work.

10. Now let's head for the heart station. (Judge whether to repeat the journey, using attentiveness and level of understanding as your guides.)

Connect

Ask students what important notes they should make in their science journals about the work of the circulatory system. Develop statements similar to these:

1. This delivery system works twenty-four hours a day.

2. It goes to every part of your body, the very tips of your toes and fingers, all through your legs and your middle, up and down your arms, into your neck and up through your head.

3. The blood carries nutrients and oxygen to cells and removes carbon dioxide.

4. The cells use the nutrients and oxygen to make energy, and energy keeps the body working.

5. The heart is the pump that makes this delivery system work.

➤ Activity Plan 5: Protecting the Body—Skin

Materials

Ten-pound weight (Use whatever you have to create the ten-pound weight—a bag of books, a box of paper, a bag of flour, etc.)
Masking tape rectangle measuring eleven feet by two feet marked on the floor (see figure 7.8)
Piece of rubber
Piece of elastic

How many layers?

Draw and label a picture that shows the layers of the skin. Be sure to include these parts:

top layer	sweat pore
second layer	nerve ending
living skin	hair
dead skin	

How strong is your hair?

Find out about hair and write a paragraph sharing your information:

1. How fast does it grow?
2. What is the main ingredient in hair? (What is hair made of?)
3. What determines the color of your hair?

Develop an experiment that shows the strength of hair.

1. What comparison material will you use? Will it be fishing line, cotton thread, or nylon thread?
2. Does it matter what the color of your hair is? Is dark hair stronger than red hair?
3. Be sure to ask an adult for help when cutting a strand or two or your hair.

Did you know?

Draw and label a picture that shows the parts of a fingernail and how it is attached to your finger. Be sure to include these parts:

end of the nail	nail bed
body of the nail	fingertip
cuticle	the "half-moons"

How fast do nails grow?
I know nails (claws) in animals help them run, climb, and hunt. Why do I have nails?

►Figure 7.8. Discovery Investigations

Magnifying lens (One per student; folding magnifiers available from Delta Education, P.O. Box 3000, Nashua, NH 03061-3000; cost: $2.00 each.)
Science journals
Transparency of the covering system discovery investigations (see figure 7.8)

Engage

Gather students around the masking tape rectangle on the floor and use the riddle to introduce the protection systems of the body. Slowly recite the lines of the riddle in figure 7.9 to allow think time, then ask for suggested answers when you are finished with the lines. (If you need them, additional clues are: Sweat pores are located in this organ, sunburn is a danger to the health of this organ.) (*Verbal/Linguistic Intelligence*)

I'm the heaviest organ in the body.

In most adults I weigh about ten pounds (lift the ten-pound weight),
    but I can weigh up to fifteen pounds.

Protection is my job.

If I were stretched out (slowly walk the perimeter of the rectangle),
    I would cover an area that's about twenty-two square feet
    in size.

What am I?

(*the skin*)

➤ Figure 7.9. What Am I?

Elaborate

Have students take turns lifting the ten-pound weight. Stretch the piece of elastic and manipulate the piece of rubber to illustrate how the skin provides a tough, elastic, waterproof covering for the body.

Ask the students: Is your skin all the same? (Invite speculation and discussion, then have students use the magnifying lenses and spend time examining and observing their skin in a variety of places: arms, wrists, fingertips, palms, legs, soles.) What differences do you notice? Which skin area is smoothest? (*Logical/Mathematical and Bodily/Kinesthetic Intelligences*)

Pose the question: What are the important jobs of the skin? Allow time for students to discuss their ideas with partners and to conduct some research. When they share discussion and research results, have them develop statements similar to the following and record the information in their science journals:

1. The skin protects the body from germs and bacteria.

2. The skin keeps the body from drying out.

3. The skin helps keep your temperature just right; when you get hot, you sweat through the pores of the skin, and when the sweat dries, you cool off.

4. The skin tells the body about its surroundings; it uses the senses of touch, heat, cold, and pain. (*Verbal/Linguistic and Interpersonal Intelligences*)

Explore

Use the transparency of figure 7.8 (covering system discovery center investigations) to show students the choices for research. Have students work with partners, select one investigation, and prepare the product for the class. (*Visual/Spatial, Verbal/Linguistic, Logical/Mathematical, and Interpersonal Intelligences*)

Connect

Have students present the products from the discovery center investigations.

➤ Activity Plan 6: Protecting the Body—Bones

Materials

Science journals
Transparency of figure 7.10 (Bones of the Body)
Activity sheet 7.1, Body Template (One per student; students will use this body template to identify the bones of the body.)
Marrow bone (available at grocery stores)
Paper samples that can be rolled into cylinders (various thicknesses, textures, lengths, and heights)
Scissors
Transparent tape (several rolls)
Activity sheet 7.2, Cylinder Investigation Sheet (multiple copies)

Text continues on page 152.

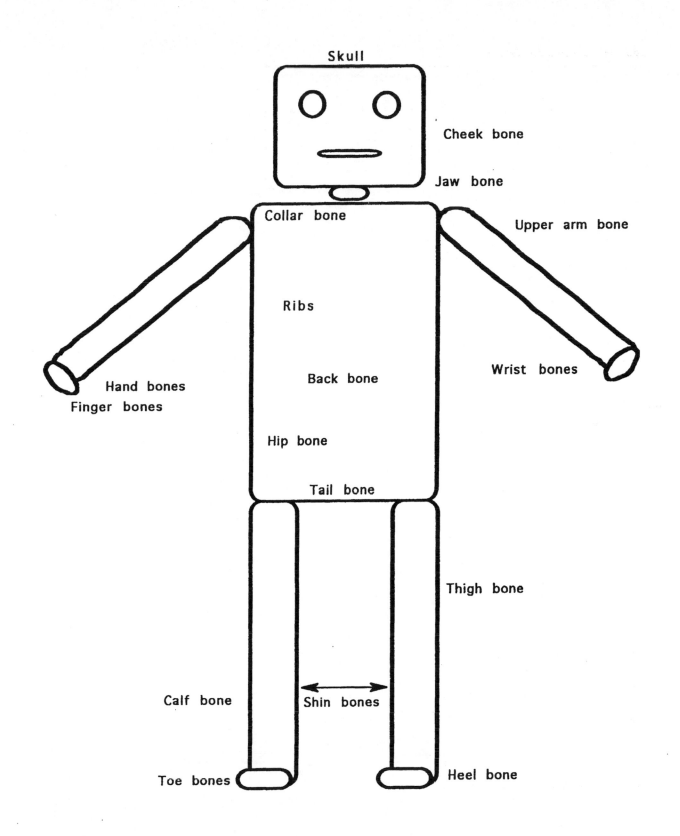

➤ Figure 7.10. Bones of the Body

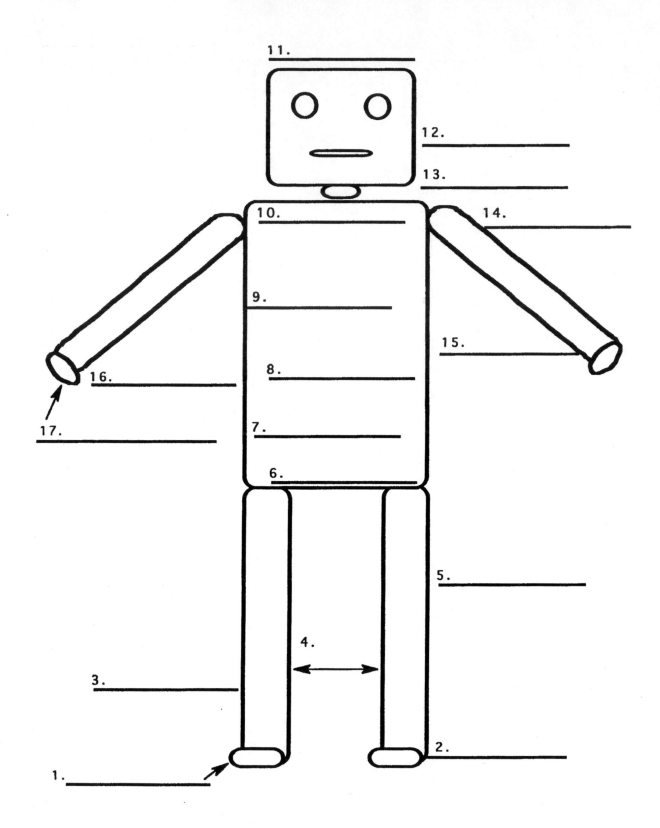

➤ Activity Sheet 7.1. Body Template

How Strong Is a Cylinder?

1. Design a cylinder.

2. Measure the cylinder and record the measurements here:

Height: Diameter:

3. How much weight can it hold before it buckles?

4. Describe your process. Talk about the thickness of the paper, whether the cylinder was vertical or horizontal, how you placed the weights, and how it buckled.

5. Re-design your cylinder.

6. What are the new measurements?

Height: Diameter:

7. How much weight can it hold before it buckles?

8. Describe your changes. Talk about the thickness of the paper, whether the cylinder was vertical or horizontal, how you placed the weights, and how it buckled.

➤ Activity Sheet 7.2. Cylinder Investigation Sheet

Engage

Display the transparency listing the bones of the body. As you review the bones, have students feel and manipulate the bones of their bodies (*Bodily/Kinesthetic Intelligence*):

1. Let's start with the bones of the feet. (Have students remove their shoes and flex their toes, then gently use their hands to squeeze and feel the toe bones, the arches of their feet, and the heel bones.)

2. Now let's move to the shin bone and the calf bone. The shin bone is found on the inner side of the lower leg and the calf bone is found on the outer side of the lower leg. Remember gently, gently feel for the bones. (Have students find the separation between the bones by running a hand up the front of the lower leg, then feeling for the shin bone on the inner side and the calf bone on the outside.)

3. Thigh bones are difficult to feel because you have so much muscle! These bones reach from your kneecap to the base of your hip bone. (Show this.)

4. Can you feel your hip bone? (Have students gently squeeze lower sides to find hip bones.)

5. If you reach around to the middle of your back to the tail of your spine, you'll find the tail bone.

6. Leave the tail bone, but follow a straight path up the middle of your back; as you trace this path, you are feeling the bones of your spine, or vertebrae.

7. Gently hold your rib cage and take some deep breaths. What happens? (Rib cages move up and down as students inhale and exhale.)

8. Go back to your spine as it reaches your upper body and moves through your neck to your skull. Feel your skull. What do you notice? (The bones seem fused.)

9. Gently feel your cheek bones, then open and close your mouth several times. What do you notice? (The bones are hinged, which allows them to open and close their mouths.)

10. We're almost done. Let's turn to our arms. Start at your shoulders: Do you feel your collar bones? They really feel bony and not very well protected.

11. Move your hands from your shoulders to your wrists, from the upper arm bone, which may be difficult to feel because of your muscles, to the lower arm bones, then to your wrist bones.

12. Flex and move your hands; here you find your hand and finger bones. Compare them to your toe and heel bones. What do you notice? (They're jointed, and they sort of feel the same.)

13. There you are—the bones of the body. (As you dramatize the rhyme, pause each time after the word connected, to let students identify the next bone. The dramatization, with the pauses, will help students visualize the bones of the body.)

Review the bones with students by reciting the old rhyme: "The toe bone's (touch your toes) connected to the heel bone (touch your heels), the heel bone's connected to the ankle bone (touch your ankles), the ankle bone's connected to the shin bone (touch your shins), the shin bone's connected to the thigh bone (pat your thighs), the thigh bone's connected to the hip bone (pat your hip bones), the hip bone's connected to the back bone (can you feel it?), the back bone's connected to the skull bone (pat your skull)." Ask the students what you forgot. (the arm and hand bones) Start again: "The collar bone's connected to the arm bone (touch your collar bones), the arm bone's connected to the wrist bone (touch your wrist bones), the wrist bone's connected to the hand bone (flex your hands), and the hand bone's connected to the finger bones (stretch those fingers)."

Elaborate

Have students work with partners, using activity sheet 7.1, to identify the bones of the body. Remind them to think about the rhyme and to use their fingers to feel the various bones, if they are stumped. Circulate as they work and reinforce the directions by dramatizing parts of the rhyme as they are needed. If everyone seems to be struggling, repeat the whole rhyme and ask students to participate. (*Interpersonal Intelligence*)

Next, discuss the bones' functions with the students: We've focused on naming the bones of the body, but what's the job of the bones? (support the body, protect the body, help the body move, make red blood cells) Have students record these jobs in their science journals. Continue: If we didn't have bones we would be like rag dolls, limp and very floppy. (Have students stand, lean over, and flop arms, pretending to be rag dolls.)

Ask the students: What needs protecting inside the body? (organs of the body) Have students feel their skulls. Ask them what the skull protects. (brain) Have students inhale and exhale several times, then ask them what the rib cage protects (lungs and heart) and what the back bones (spine) protects (spinal cord).

Next, ask students how the bones help in movement. (If they were all one piece, we wouldn't be able to bend or sit or lie down easily.) Have students bend arms, legs, and fingers several times to explore movements allowed by the joints of the body.

Explain that a fourth job of the bones is to make red blood cells: This happens inside the bones in the marrow (show the marrow bone from the grocery store and point out the marrow). There are special cells in the bone marrow that produce the red blood cells you need, about 200 billion of them every day!

Explore

Explain to the students: The long bones of your legs and arms are really cylinders. Scientists have discovered that cylinders have greater strength than solid rods. We will explore this strength with some experimentation. On the table are different paper samples; some are long and some are short and they vary in thickness. Your job is to roll a cylinder and experiment with how much weight it can hold. You may have fat cylinders, skinny cylinders, tall or short cylinders, cylinders within cylinders; you decide. Tape is also available as you roll the cylinders; use it wisely and carefully. Use the cylinder investigation sheet to guide your investigations (activity sheet 7.2). (*Logical/Mathematical and Bodily/Kinesthetic Intelligences*)

Connect

Have students share the results of their cylinder investigations. Ask them to identify which design worked most effectively and why.

➤ Activity Plan 7: Control— Messages to and from the Brain

Materials

Clock with a second hand
Science journals

Engage

Have students stand in a large circle and hold hands. Select one student as the "starter" and test the group's reaction times: When you say "go" (and begin watching the second hand of the clock), the starter should immediately squeeze the left hand of the person next in the circle, and that person should squeeze the left hand of the next person, and on around the circle until the starter feels the squeeze and shouts "stop." How much time did it take?

Repeat the experiment to see if practice improves the reaction times. (*Bodily/Kinesthetic Intelligence*)

Elaborate

Ask the students: What system of the body was necessary for this experiment to work successfully? (nervous system) How does this system work? (Use the experiment and figure 7.11 to identify the parts of the system and explain how it works.)

➤ Figure 7.11. A Message to the Brain

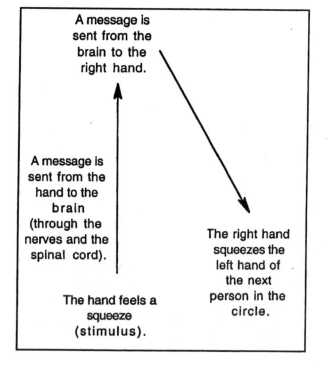

A message is sent from the brain to the right hand.

A message is sent from the hand to the brain (through the nerves and the spinal cord).

The right hand squeezes the left hand of the next person in the circle.

The hand feels a squeeze (stimulus).

Tell the students that the control center of the nervous system is the brain (protected by the skull); at the base of the brain is the brain stem, just above the neck. The brain stem attaches to the spinal cord (protected by the back bone), and nerves branch out from the spinal cord to all parts of the body (see figure 7.12).

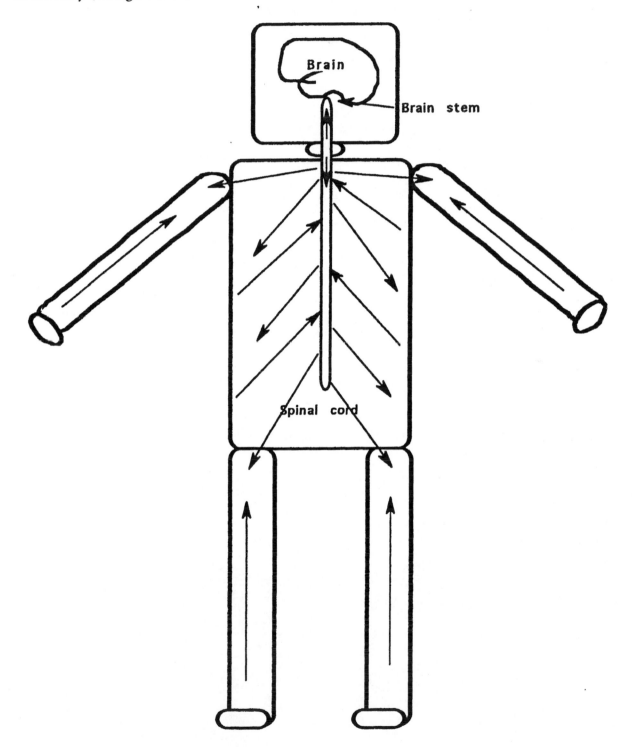

➤ Figure 7.12. The Nervous System

The nerves are the pathways that send and receive messages from the brain; this is how we were able to conduct our reaction time experiment. Through the sense of touch, the brain received the message that the left hand was squeezed, it sent a return message that made the right hand squeeze the next student's left hand, and the message continued around the circle. Ask the students: What are other ways the brain senses its surroundings? (sight, hearing, taste, smell)

Explore

Have students work with partners to choose one of the senses and create an activity for the class. Activities should help students explore the abilities of the senses. See figure 7.13 if students are stumped for ideas. (*Interpersonal Intelligence*)

Exploring the Five Senses	
Sight	Optical illusions, the effects of light on the pupil, blinking reactions, seeing 3-D images
Hearing	Radio skits with lots of sound effects, direction of sound experiments, materials that conduct sound, musical patterns, softest sound you can hear, balancing
Taste	Name that taste, sweet and sour tastes, how salty is it?
Smell	Name that smell (herbs and spices), sneezing (why it happens)
Touch	Read Braille, match the adjectives (rough, smooth, hot, cold), what object is it?

Exploring Learning and Memory
Games (like chess, checkers, battleship), jigsaw puzzles, logic puzzles, memory games, dance patterns

➤ Figure 7.13. Exploring the Five Senses

Connect

Set up the activity centers the students have planned and devote an afternoon to exploring the activities. At the close of the afternoon have students reflect in their science journals and make generalizations about the nervous system. Some responses may be: The brain is the control center of the nervous system, messages travel to and from the brain through the nerves and the spinal cord, the five senses (sight, hearing, taste, touch, smell) bring information to the brain from the environment, the brain makes memories from our learning experiences.

➤ Activity Plan 8: Coordination—The Muscles of the Body

Materials

Science journals

Engage

Repeat the body movements from the opening lesson when *Song and Dance Man* was introduced (see page 134). (*Bodily/Kinesthetic Intelligence*)

Elaborate

Ask students: What system of the body helped us make these movements? (the muscular system) Muscles are responsible for every movement in the body, whether you are running, writing, digesting food, or making your heart beat faster. All of the actions happen because of the three kinds of muscles in our bodies: skeletal, smooth, and cardiac. What controls the muscles of the body? (The brain sends electrical signals to the muscles, which makes them react.)

Explore

Write *skeletal, smooth, cardiac, voluntary,* and *involuntary* on the board and begin to explore understanding of these words with the students (*Bodily/Kinesthetic Intelligence*):

1. Let's look at our skeletal muscles first. Locate the bicep and tricep muscles of your arms. (Bicep muscles are located on the front of the upper arm and tricep muscles are located on the back of the upper arm.) Rest your elbows on your desks and slowly raise and lower your forearms. What happens to the bicep and tricep muscles? (The bicep muscle contracts—tightens and gets shorter—and pulls the arm to a raised position. The tricep muscle relaxes. When the arm is lowered, the bicep muscle relaxes and the tricep muscle contracts: tightens and gets shorter.)

2. Another skeletal muscle pair can be found in the upper legs, in the muscles of the thighs. The quadricep muscle is located on the front of your upper thigh and the hamstring muscle is located on the back of the upper thigh. Stand beside your desks and slowly raise and lower your legs (with knees bent). What happens to the two muscles? (The quadricep muscle contracts and pulls the leg to a raised position as the hamstring muscle relaxes. When the leg is lowered, the quadricep muscle relaxes and the hamstring muscle contracts.)

3. Are these movements voluntary or involuntary movements? (voluntary) Why? (You make them work when you want to.) Why are these muscles called skeletal muscles? (They are joined to the bones of the skeleton.) These muscles work under the control of the brain; for example, if you want to brush your hair, your brain cells send a message through the spinal cord and the motor nerves to the muscles of your arm and fingers. The message tells the muscles of the fingers to contract to grasp the brush and the muscles of the arm to contract to raise the arm. The message system is so efficient that just the right amount of strength is used to grasp the brush and lift the arm to brush the hair.

4. The muscles of the face and the hands are fun to explore. Turn to a partner and watch each other smile, frown, grimace, raise and lower eyebrows, and move tongues. All of these movements are controlled by muscles. What movements of the hand can you identify? (grasp, grab, hold, squeeze, clench, pinch, flick, draw, write) Are these movements of the face and hand voluntary or involuntary? (voluntary)

5. What are involuntary muscles of the body? (These are the muscles that we cannot control because they work automatically.) Can you think of some examples? (The muscles of the heart and the stomach are two examples.) Smooth muscles in the esophagus, the stomach, and the intestines contract to squeeze the food you have eaten and push it forward. These muscles work automatically. Smooth muscles also control the width of your air passages in your breathing system, and muscles in the walls of your blood vessels can narrow and expand to control your blood pressure. These are also involuntary. Even in the waste disposal system, smooth muscles automatically work to keep urine flowing from the kidneys into the bladder. Your heart muscle (the third kind of muscle) is the strongest muscle of all because it has to contract and relax at least seventy times a minute (for an adult). This muscle works even when you are sleeping.

6. Can you think of involuntary muscles that can also be voluntary, at least for a short period of time? (your breathing muscles and the muscles that control blinking) Take a deep breath and hold your breath to the count of five, then stare at each other without blinking. Most of the time we are not aware of these breathing and blinking movements.

7. What builds strong, healthy muscles? (exercise and protein-rich foods) Have students conduct research to make a list of protein-rich foods. (meats, fish, vegetables, grains)

8. Write these words on the board: *largest, smallest, longest, most powerful, strongest.* Address the students again: The largest muscle in our body is the gluteus maximus, and it's located in the buttocks. It helps us jump. The smallest muscle in the

body, the stapedius muscle, is located in the ear and controls sound vibrations if the sound is too loud. The longest muscle starts at your waist and crosses diagonally down across your thigh to your inner knee; it's called the sartorius muscle. The most powerful muscles are found in your head. Can you identify where they are? (the jaw muscles, because they clamp your jaws closed when you are chewing) We discussed the strongest muscle; what is it? (heart muscle)

Connect

Have students use their science journals to make generalizations about muscles. Some statements may be: Muscles move our bodies; voluntary muscles are muscles that we can control, and skeletal muscles are voluntary muscles; involuntary muscles are muscles that work automatically such as the heart muscle and smooth muscles; the brain sends messages through the spinal cord and the motor nerves to tell muscles when and how to move; if you exercise and eat protein-rich foods, then you build and keep healthy muscles.

➤ Activity Plan 9: Generations

Materials

Science journals
Transparency of figure 7.14 (Generations)
Activity sheet 7.3, Traits of Students (multiple copies)

Engage

Have students use their science journals to draw the life cycle of a human: egg, infant, child, young adult, adult (see figure 7.14).

Elaborate

Show the transparency of figure 7.14 and pose this question: What system of the body allows humans to produce children, grandchildren, great-grandchildren, great-great-grandchildren, and so on into the future? (reproductive) Through the reproductive system we inherit characteristics of our family: hair color, eye color, height, bone structure, blood type—all kinds of characteristics are passed down from generation to generation.

Explore

Have students survey each other to discover some of the characteristics of the class: eye colors, hair colors, ear lobes (attached or unattached), and the ability to curl the tongue. Use activity sheet 7.3 to record the information.

Text continues on page 162.

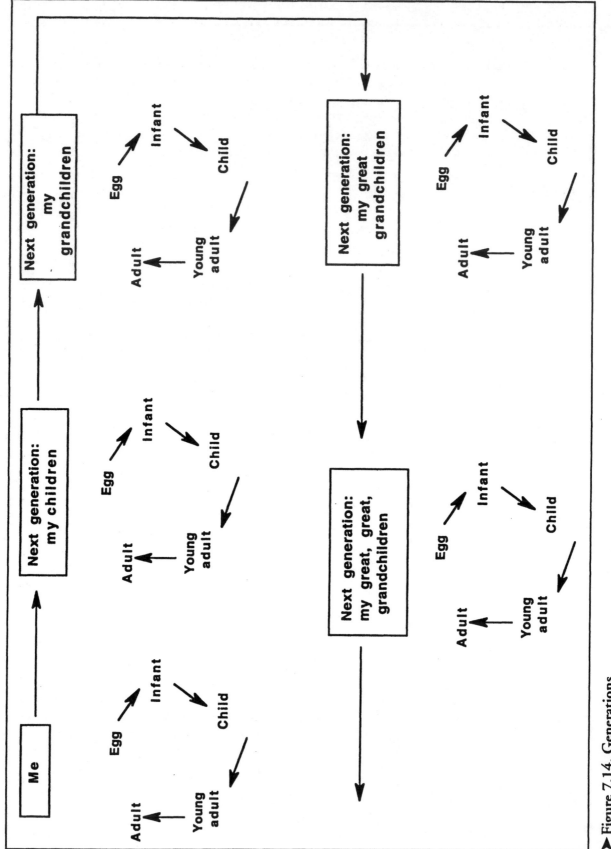

▶ Figure 7.14. Generations

Traits of Students

| Student | Eye Color | Hair Color | Tongue Curling | | Ear Lobes | |
			Yes	No	Attached	Unattached

➤ Activity Sheet 7.3. Traits of Students

Connect

Have students use their science journals to make generalizations about the reproductive system. Some responses may be: The reproductive system helps human beings produce new human beings, we inherit many characteristics of our parents.

➤ Culminating Activity Plan: Stage a Vaudeville Show

Have students organize and present a vaudeville show. Think about what they might bring to this show. Vaudeville shows had dancers (tap and soft shoe), jugglers, singers, magicians, and comedians. Students may work together or individually; encourage them to wear costumes and gather any props that might enhance their performances. (*Bodily/Kinesthetic Intelligence*)

8   A Story, a Story

Retold by Gail E. Haley
Illustrated by Gail E. Haley
New York: Atheneum, 1970

Summary

➤ Little Ananse, the spider man, matches wits with Nyame the Sky God to
bring the golden box of stories back to Earth to the people of his village.
He spins a web to the sky and hears the price for the stories: He must bring
the Sky God Osebo the leopard, Mmboro the hornet, and Mmoatia the fairy.
A game with vine creepers captures the leopard, a calabash and a banana
leaf fool the hornets, and a doll covered with sticky latex gum catches the
fairy. Ananse spins a second web and pulls his captives to the feet of the
Sky God; he receives the stories and returns to his village to scatter the
stories to the corners of the world.

Award Year

➤ 1971

Art Information

➤ Illustrated using woodcuts.

Curriculum Connections

➤ Spiders and insects, with emphasis on this science idea: Spiders and insects
are essential in our world: they help pollinate crops, decompose wood and
dead leaves, feed other animals, control pests, and provide products (like
honey and silk) that humans use.

➤ Activity Plan 1: Sharing the Story

Materials

African music (*African Tribal Music and Dances*, featuring the music of Malinke, Baoule, and others, from Delta Music, 1993, is a good selection, available at a music store.)

Golden story box (We covered a dress or suit box, i.e., a box with a hinged lid, with gold wrapping paper.)

Your own special box or treasure chest (I brought a wooden box that held audiotapes of my son's first efforts at talking and other treasures from his childhood.)

Caldecott Award poster

Rubber stamp of some kind

Ink pad

Small block of soft wood (balsa or pine)

Knife

Engage

Play the music and show students the box in which you keep special memories. Quiet the music and ask students to share special things they might store in such a box. Share what you have in the box. (*Musical/Rhythmic and Verbal/Linguistic Intelligences*)

Elaborate

Share the introduction to the story. Ask the students what the purpose of a spider story is. (Spider stories are trickster stories and show small, defenseless characters using trickery to outwit others and succeed against great odds.)

Provide focus for listening: Ask students to speculate about how Ananse might defend himself in encounters with a leopard, hornets, and a fairy. Refocus question: What would be dangers from the animals and the fairy? (He would have to worry about the leopard's claws, speed, and climbing abilities; the hornets' swarming and stinging characteristics; and the possibility that the fairy might be hard to find, or when found, might cast a spell on him.)

Explore

Share the story.

Connect

Ask the students: How did Ananse outwit the leopard, the hornets, and the fairy? How would you trick them? Ananse brought the stories back to Earth, opened the box, and scattered the stories to the corners of the world, then invited readers to "let some come back to me." Show the golden box that will be used to hold the stories the students write.

The introduction to the story said that some words and phrases would be repeated several times. Ask the students what the repeated words were and how they make the story stronger. Some answers might be: twe, twe, twe (laughter): really funny that Ananse wanted to buy the stories and that such a weak old man could gladly pay the price; so small, so small, so small: very very small; yiridi, yiridi, yiridi: running; binding binding game and your foot and foot: he will really tie up the leopard; by his foot, by his foot, by his foot, by his foot: really tied up; raining, raining, raining: hornets like to get out of the rain, if it were only a few drops, they might not be fooled; dancing, dancing, dancing: always moving; eeeee, eeeee, eeeee: pleased by his success.

Share the Caldecott Award information:

1. As students examine the cover of the book, ask them what special thing they notice. (gold medal) Ask them what the name of the medal is. (Caldecott Award Medal) Ask them why it has been placed on this book. (Some responses may be: The illustrations are special, well done, particularly interesting, exciting, and/or unusual.)

2. Discuss the art techniques used in creating the pictures. Gail Haley used woodcuts to illustrate the story. Show and use the rubber stamp to help students understand the process of illustrating with woodcuts. The wood is carved so the areas to be printed are raised from the wood that will not be printed. (Show the huts on the first page.) When the woodcuts are inked and printed, often the grain of the wood is visible. (Show the wall behind Ananse on the first page of the story and several of the illustrations showing Ananse.)

3. Ask two student volunteers to search the poster for the year the story won. (Searching the poster helps students become familiar with the many different titles selected for the award.)

➤ Activity Plan 2: Writing Our Own Trickster Stories

Materials

Golden box from the introductory lesson
African music (see Activity Plan 1)

Engage

Set the mood for students by again playing the African music. As the music plays softly, help students brainstorm ideas for original Ananse stories using a spider or insect as the Ananse character. (*Musical/Rhythmic Intelligence*)

Elaborate

Address the class: You have been asked to contribute stories to the golden box of stories. What will be your story? Before we begin, let's look more closely at this trickster story and some other examples.

Make a five-column chart on the board and label the columns. Ask the students: Who is the trickster? Who is tricked? Why? What is the trick? What is the result? Based on *A Story, A Story*, have the class fill in the chart. (See figure 8.1.)

Share the other examples to reinforce the characteristics of trickster tales and to model various ways they could develop:

- In the second example Anansi (spelled with an "i" this time) is hungry and wanders as he thinks how to get his dinner. When he comes upon a moss-covered stone he is puzzled and remarks, "What's a moss-covered stone doing here?" Immediately he falls to the ground, stunned; when this happens several times, he eventually realizes this is a magical stone and he can use it to trick other animals. He brings several animals to the stone, gets them to say the magic question, and while they are stunned, he steals their food supplies and has a wonderful dinner.

- In the third example, Ananse is again hungry but too lazy to work for his dinner. This time he tricks Granny Anika. Granny Anika loves to dance, in fact her nickname is "The Dancing Granny," and as soon as she hears music she begins to tap her feet and move her body. Ananse sings to her, and as she dances away from her vegetable fields, he takes food (corn and peas) home to his family.

- In the fourth example, Zomo is a rabbit who seeks wisdom from the Sky God. The price for wisdom includes scales from Big Fish, milk from the wild cow, and a tooth from a leopard. With a drum Zomo makes Big Fish dance until he loses his scales. With laughter, Zomo angers the wild cow, who tries to fell the tree where Zomo is hiding; the cow's horns get stuck in the tree and Zomo milks her. With some spilled milk and some scattered fish scales, Zomo causes leopard to slip and roll down a hill and bump his face on a rock, knocking loose a tooth. Zomo takes the three items to the Sky God and receives his wisdom.

Have the class use insects and spiders as the trickster characters in the stories they create for the golden box. Create a new five-column chart and brainstorm some ideas. List students ideas; see figure 8.2 if the class is stumped.

Ask the students: What insects and spiders might we choose as our trickster characters? Who will they trick and why? What do they want? What will be the trick? And what will the result be?

Explore

Have students choose an idea from the prewrite chart or think of another idea and write the first drafts of their stories. Once rough drafts are complete, have students share their stories with partners, then make revisions to be sure they have the trickster story characteristics: lots of detail and clearly defined beginnings, middles, and ends. Make editing corrections (spelling, capitalization, and punctuation) and write or type final copies and place stories in the golden box.

Text continues on page 169.

Who is the trickster?	Who is tricked?	Why?	What is the trick?	What is the result?
Ananse	Leopard, hornet, fairy	Ananse wants stories from Sky God.	A game, the threat of rain, and a wooden doll who will not talk.	Ananse received the golden box of stories from Sky God and brought them back to the people of his village.
Anansi	Lion, elephant, giraffe, zebra	Anansi is hungry but too lazy to work for his dinner.	A strange, moss-covered rock.	Anansi gets lots of yams and bananas and squash for his dinner.
Ananse	Granny Anika	Ananse is hungry but too lazy to work for his dinner.	Ananse sings and Granny breaks into dance as she hears it.	Ananse takes food to his family: corn and peas.
Zomo	Big fish, wild cow, leopard	Zomo wants Sky God to give him wisdom.	A drum, laughter and a tree, spilled milk, and a rock.	Zomo receives wisdom from Sky God.

▶ Figure 8.1. Trickster Stories

Who is the trickster?	Who is tricked?	Why?	What is the trick?	What is the result?
Spider	Frog	The day is too hot and spider is comfortably resting in her web, but she really wants a drop of water to drink.	Spider tricks frog into thinking a passing cloud is a hungry heron, ready to gobble him up.	Frog jumps from the lily pad and splashes water into spider's web.
Walkingstick	Robin	Walkingstick has always wanted to fly like a bird.	Walkingstick settles on a twig that robin wants for her nest; because walking stick looks like a stick, robin doesn't even notice him.	Walkingstick gets to fly and then safely walks away.
Trapdoor spider	Grasshopper	Trapdoor spider wants a tasty berry but does not want to leave the safety of her burrow.	Trapdoor spider challenges grasshopper to a jumping contest.	Grasshopper knocks the berry from the bush and trapdoor has her dinner.

▶ Figure 8.2. Ideas for Original Trickster Stories

Connect

Begin the village ceremony (gather in a circle on the floor), play the African music, and pass the golden box (as if playing musical chairs or the game "hot potato"). When the music stops, the student holding the golden box opens the box and selects a story to read to the class. Continue sharing in this manner until all have had opportunities to read stories.

➤ Activity Plan 3: How Do They Compare?

Materials

Insects for observation (Available at local pet shops or from an educational supply house like Delta Education, P.O. Box 915, Hudson, NH 03051, 1-800-258-1302. Delta has praying mantis pods, painted lady butterfly larvae, ants, ladybugs, crickets, and mealworm beetles.)

Science journals

Activity sheet 8.1, Observation Chart (multiple copies for each insect that will be observed)

Chart paper

Engage

Introduce the insects for observation and let student groups gather around the containers to watch and draw what they see, using their science journals. (*Naturalist and Visual/Spatial Intelligences*)

Elaborate

Use the chart paper to create a comparison chart of facts about insects and spiders. Divide the class into two groups. Group one looks for spider facts and group two looks for insect facts (see figure 8.3). After discussing metamorphoses, ask students to observe the insects and identify their life cycle stages. (*Logical/Mathematical Intelligence*)

Explore

Have the students select favorite insects or spiders and use the discovery centers to investigate the lives and behaviors of the insects or spiders. (*Verbal/Linguistic, Visual/Spatial, and Bodily/Kinesthetic Intelligences*)

Connect

Set up a schedule for insect observations and assign two students per insect per day; have them use the observation sheets (activity sheet 8.1) to draw daily pictures and note any changes in the insects.

Text continues on page 172.

Insect:	Date:
	Time:

Picture:

Changes:

➤Activity Sheet 8.1. Observation Chart

Insects	Spiders
Six jointed legs	Eight jointed legs
Three body parts: head, thorax, abdomen	Two body parts: head, abdomen
Simple and compound eyes	Simple eyes
Wings	No wings
Antennae	No antennae
Two main types of mouthparts, which allow them to chew, bite, lap, or suck	No biting mouth parts
Invertebrate	Invertebrate
Exoskeleton, which sheds so insect can grow larger	Exoskeleton, which sheds so spider can grow larger
Life cycles: complete metamorphoses (egg, larva, pupa, adult) or incomplete metamorphoses (egg, nymph, adult)	Life cycle: (egg, spiderling, adult)
Found on all continents	Found on all continents except Antarctica
	Poison fangs Several pairs of spinnerets to produce silk for webs

►Figure 8.3. Comparison Chart: Insects and Spiders

When the discovery center investigations are complete, have students present their application, synthesis, and evaluation products.

MY FAVORITE INSECT

Knowledge
Choose a favorite insect and research to find its diet, body structures, habitat, life cycle, interesting behaviors, and contribution to the world (pollination, pest control, food source, product humans use, and/or decomposition of wood and leaves). Make a sketch of the insect and label its body parts.

Comprehension
Does your insect have a life cycle of complete metamorphosis or incomplete metamorphosis? Make and label a drawing that illustrates the metamorphosis of your insect. Identify the insect's diet at the larva and adult stages of life and add that information to your drawing; for example, a butterfly sucks juices from flowers, but as a caterpillar it's a chewing creature and nibbles and eats leaves.

Application
Make a model of the insect. *Hint:* Think about "found" materials that you could use, like fabric scraps, nature materials (nuts, grasses, sticks, pinecones), string, yarn, toothpicks, small boxes, or paper cups.

Analysis
Meet with two other students to share your body structure models and the drawings you made identifying the body parts of your insects or spiders (from your application and knowledge steps). How are your insects and spiders different? Make a list of some of these differences.

Synthesis
Review the list of differences you made during the "analysis" step. Change the look of your insect, turning it into a cartoon critter that combines at least three differences from your list. Give your cartoon critter a name and create a caption for the picture. For example, if you were a ladybug, your cartoon ladybug might have the body of a walking stick, the eight legs of a spider, and a home in a web.

Evaluation
Evaluate the insect's contribution to the world: Does it help pollinate crops, decompose wood and dead leaves, feed people or other animals, control pests, and/or provide a product that humans use? Use an index card to write about the contributions of the insect to the world. Display your insect model and place the index card in front of the insect.

MY FAVORITE SPIDER

Knowledge
Choose a favorite spider and research its diet, body structures, habitat, life cycle, interesting behaviors, and contribution to the world (pollination, pest control, food source, product humans use, and/or decomposition of wood and leaves). Make a sketch of the spider and label its body parts.

Comprehension
Make a drawing illustrating the habitat and web of your spider. Identify its diet and add that information to your drawing; for example, the European fishing spider lives most of its life underwater in an airtight diving bell web that moves from the surface of the water, where the spider takes in air, down to the underwater plants. It catches mites, insect larvae, and other prey living on the underwater plants.

Application
Make a model of the spider. *Hint*: Think about "found" materials that you could use, like fabric scraps, nature materials (nuts, grasses, sticks, pinecones), string, yarn, toothpicks, small boxes, or paper cups.

Analysis
Meet with two other students to share your body structure models and the drawings you made identifying the body parts of your insects or spiders (from your application and knowledge steps). How are your insects and spiders different? Make a list of some of these differences.

Synthesis
Review the list of differences you made during the "analysis" step. Change the look of your spider, turning it into a cartoon critter that combines at least three differences from your list. Give your cartoon critter a name and create a caption for the picture. For example, if you were a tarantula, your cartoon tarantula might have three body parts instead of two, antennae, and a home in a hive.

Evaluation
Evaluate the spider's contribution to the world: How does it control pests? Use an index card to write about its usefulness. Display your spider model and place the index card in front of the spider.

9   *Sylvester and the Magic Pebble*

Written by William Steig
Illustrated by William Steig
New York: Windmill Books, 1969

Summary

➤ A young donkey named Sylvester finds a magic pebble and discovers that it will grant his every wish as long as he is holding it. But to his dismay, a frightening encounter with a lion causes him to panic and make a wish to be a rock. He spends a year as a rock—through all the seasons and through all kinds of weather—and finally in springtime returns to his true donkey self. In the end the magic pebble is stored in a very safe place.

Award Year

➤ 1970

Art Information

➤ Illustrated using watercolors.

Curriculum Connections

➤ Weather, with emphasis on this science idea: The foundations of the weather are light, air, and water. *Note*: Weather station instruments (barometer, wind vane, anemometer, and rain gauge) may be constructed by the students or purchased from Delta Education, P.O. Box 3000, Nashua, NH 03061, 800-442-5444, or Edmund Scientific Company, Consumer Science Division, 101 East Gloucester Pike, Barrington, NJ 08007, 800-728-6999.

➤ Activity Plan 1: Sharing the Story

Materials

Pebble
Chart paper
Marker
Caldecott Award poster
Pen and ink (available from art stores)
Watercolor paint (available from art stores)
Copies of the following note to parents (one per student)

Dear Parents,

As part of our weather unit, we are sharing the adventures of Sylvester from the story *Sylvester and the Magic Pebble* by William Steig. This is a delightful story about a young donkey who finds a pebble and discovers that it will grant his every wish as long as he is holding it.

To support our extension activities, please help your child find a pebble to bring to school. Please place the pebble in a plastic bag and label the bag with your child's name.

Thank you,

Engage

Show the pebble you have selected and ask students to imagine what might happen if the pebble were magical. Ask them what wishes it might grant or make happen. (*Verbal/Linguistic Intelligence*)

Elaborate

Share the story. Students should be able to answer this question after listening to the story: What happens to Sylvester's pebble?

Explore

Discuss the story by asking the students the following questions:

1. How do Mr. Steig's illustrations reinforce/emphasize the amount of time Sylvester spent as a rock? (summer, fall, winter, spring pictures) What weather conditions does Sylvester experience during the story, both as himself and as a rock? (rain when he finds the pebble; bright sunshine when he discovers its magic powers; a thunderstorm when he tests its magic powers; sunshine again as he plans his many wishes and during the first month of being a rock; cloudy, windy, cold weather as the season changes to fall; snow during the winter; warmth and sunshine as spring returns; bright sunshine for the picnic in May and his return to his true self)

2. What feelings does Sylvester experience? (As students relive the events of the story, draw a wavy line and list events to indicate the ups and downs in Sylvester's feelings. See figure 9.1.)

3. What advice would you give Sylvester to help him make a wiser choice at the beginning of the story?

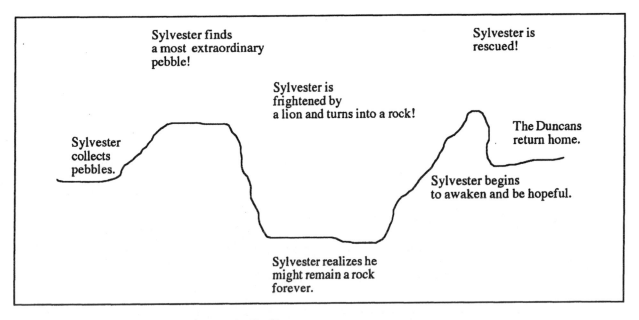

➤ Figure 9.1. Changes in Sylvester's Feelings

Connect

Share the Caldecott Award information:

1. As students examine the cover of the book, ask them what special thing they notice. (gold medal) Ask them the name of the medal. (Caldecott Award Medal) Ask them why it has been placed on this book. (Some answers might be: The illustrations are special, well done, particularly interesting, exciting, and/or unusual.)

2. Discuss the art techniques used in creating the pictures. Pen and ink create the figures and shapes, and watercolors add the variations in colors. (Browse the illustrations to notice how the watercolors are applied, particularly in the skies, in the rock, and in the landscape of the hills because it is so realistic.)

3. Ask two student volunteers to search the poster for the year the story won. (Searching the poster helps students become familiar with the many different titles selected for the award.)

Ask students to search at home and bring pebbles (one per student). Distribute the note for parents and remind students to show their parents the note when they get home.

➤ Activity Plan 2: Sorting and Classifying Pebbles

Materials

Sheet of paper (long enough so students can comfortably gather on either side of it)
Drawing paper
Illustrating materials (markers, crayons, or colored pencils)
Glue

Engage

Sort and classify the class according to a variety of criteria: hair colors, glasses/no glasses, dark shoes/light shoes, eye colors. (*Logical/Mathematical Intelligence*)

Elaborate

Gather students on either side of a long sheet of paper that has been rolled out on the floor. Have them place their pebbles in front of them on the paper. What are ways to sort and classify the pebbles? (size, color, texture [smooth, rough], shape) Sort and classify in one or two ways. Use a marker to record the results of the sorting. For example, if students are sorting by size, align the pebbles by size, then use the marker to draw around each pebble; if they are sorting by color, sort the pebbles into piles and use the marker to draw circles around each pile, then count the pebbles in each circle and write that number in the circle.

Explore

Have students use their pebbles to create pebble pictures. They should look closely at the pebbles to imagine how they could be part of the pictures—possibly a turtle's shell or the body of a seal; maybe a mushroom cap or the home of a chipmunk. Have the students use markers, crayons, or colored pencils to create the surrounding pictures and glue the pebbles in place when the pictures are completed. (*Visual/Spatial Intelligence*)

Connect

Display the pictures and have students take a museum tour. Explain "kind compliments" before the tour begins. Kind compliments are positive remarks like "neat colors," "really interesting picture," or "the pebble really fits in the picture."

➤ Activity Plan 3: What Warms Us?

Materials

    Sunny day
    Thermometers, one per student partnership
    Science journals
    Flashlight
    Globe
    Weather station instrument: thermometer

Engage

Take the students for a walk outdoors and have them use the thermometers to measure temperatures in various locations (sun and shade, open and enclosed areas) and on different surfaces (sidewalk, grass, sand, asphalt). Record the information in the science journals; be sure students note the locations and the surfaces where they measure temperatures. (*Bodily/Kinesthetic Intelligence*)

Elaborate

Discuss the temperature measurements and invite the students to speculate about the reasons for differences.

We also see these temperature differences when we look at the world. Hold the globe and ask the students what weather they think of when they look at the polar regions, either the North Pole or the South Pole. (cold, ice, snow) Ask them what it's like at the equator. (hot, wet, rainy) Ask them why the sun heats the Earth unevenly.

Darken the room and aim the flashlight directly at the board; use chalk to draw the circle it makes. Tilt the flashlight and aim its light so it hits the board at a slant; draw this circle of light. Ask the students to compare the circles. (The direct focus makes a small circle of light; the slanted focus makes a larger, oval circle of light.) Repeat the action with the flashlight and compare the intensity of the light circles. The source of light and the amount of light from the flashlight were the same, so both the oval and the circle receive the same amount of light; ask the students what they notice about the light in the oval and the light in the circle. (The oval circle of light is less bright than the direct circle of light.)

Hold the globe and aim the flashlight at the equator. Tell the students to think of the flashlight as the sun. Ask them: Which area of the world receives the most direct light? (equator) Which areas of the world receive less direct light? (the poles) The curve of the Earth causes the light to spread out near the poles. What did we say about the weather at the equator and the poles? (hot at the equator, cold at the poles) (*Logical/Mathematical Intelligence*)

Explore

Draw figure 9.2 on the board and have students draw along with you. Explain each component as you draw. Have students add this statement: *Sunshine and its uneven heating of the ground set the first stage for the weather.* (*Visual/Spatial Intelligence*)

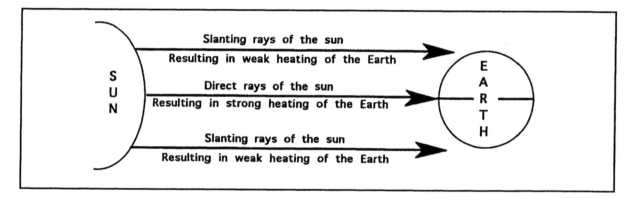

➤ Figure 9.2. The Sun's Rays and Weather

Connect

Select a location for the weather station and place the thermometer in the station. Remind students that the thermometer should be placed in the shade and ask them why that is so. (If the thermometer is in direct sunlight, the sun will warm the materials of the thermometer and show that temperature rather than the temperature of the air.)

➤ Activity Plan 4: Air Is All Around Us

Materials

Globe

Plastic bag large enough to hold the globe and retain a layer of air around it when the plastic bag is sealed (A dry cleaner's bag tied at both ends will work.)

Variety of materials for students to use in their air investigations (balloons, plastic cups, baggies, rubber bands, paper towels)

Lamp without a lampshade with at least a sixty-watt bulb in the socket

Flour

Powder puff

Weather station instruments: wind vane, barometer (optional), anemometer (optional)

Engage

Gather in one area of the classroom and lead students in a variety of breathing exercises:

1. Breathe slowly and deeply.

2. Hold your breath.

3. Run in place. What happens to your breathing? What are we breathing? How does breathing help our bodies?

Place the globe in the plastic bag and seal it (be sure a pocket of air is surrounding it) as you make this comment to the students: "The Earth is surrounded by an ocean of air. It's like an invisible skin." Ask them how we know the air is all around us. Invite speculation from students. (*Bodily/Kinesthetic and Logical/Mathematical Intelligences*)

Elaborate

Display the supplies (balloons, plastic cups, etc.) and have students work with partners to investigate ways to show the class that air is all around us. Encourage them to think of outdoor ideas too (the tug of wind on a kite, the movement of leaves and tree branches, holding a dandelion puff and watching what happens, floating objects, the movement of a sailboat). Circulate as students work, helping them think through their ideas and explanations.

Invite students to share what they have discovered and draw conclusions from the investigation (air is invisible but we can see and feel its effects).

Explore

Invite students to speculate about what makes the wind blow. Inflate a balloon and let go of the neck. Ask the students to describe what happens. (The air loudly swooshes from the balloon.) The pressure of the air inside the balloon was much higher than the surrounding air, and as soon as the neck was released, the process of evening the pressure began. The air keeps moving until the pressure inside the balloon is the same as the pressure outside the balloon. On a much larger scale this is what makes the wind blow on the Earth's surface. When the pressure between two places on the Earth's surface is different, movement of air happens as the wind blows to even the pressure, just like the balloon example.

Do another demonstration of the movement of air using the lamp and the flour. Ask the students: We have the lamp plugged in, but we haven't actually turned it on; when we do, what will be the temperature change? (The bulb will get hot and heat the surrounding air.) Use the powder puff to sprinkle some flour just above the lamp and watch it settle. Light the lamp, wait a moment or two until the bulb is hot and has heated the air surrounding it, then sprinkle some more flour just above the lamp. Ask the students to describe what happens this time. (Instead of settling, the flour particles rise.) Ask the students why this happened. (Before we lit the lamp, the air was cooler and moving downward, so the flour settled; after we lit the lamp, the air was heated and rising, so the flour dust also rose.) Heat warms the air, the warm air rises, and as it rises it cools and begins to sink.

Have students do the following exercises with partners to demonstrate this movement of warm air and cool air in the Northern Hemisphere.

Warm Air Movements

Instructions to students: Crouch with your palms held together, elbows tucked close to your sides. Spiral (turn) counterclockwise, then slowly rise and extend your arms to a "V" with palms turning outward.

Cool Air Movements

Instructions to students: Stand with your arms extended above your head in a "V" with your palms facing downward. Keep your arms extended but shift your palms so they face inward, then slowly shift to a crouching position, lowering your arms as you do. Spiral (turn) clockwise as the air moves out.

Practice the movements first, having each student try both motions; when the movements are smoothly completed, have students join with partners and explore the movements together. Partners should stand side by side, allowing a foot of space between them. The student representing cool air will extend arms upward with palms facing out (arms will form a "V"), and the student representing warm air will crouch with palms held together, elbows tucked close to the student's sides. On the count of three have students begin air movements and continue air movements through several up and down exchanges. (They will bump into each other, probably begin to giggle, and continue to bump each other as they move up and down.)

Discuss what happened. (As air currents of different sizes move at different speeds, the bumping and churning that happened to the students happens to the air currents.) Draw figure 9.3 on the board and have students use their science journals to draw along with you. Explain each component as you draw. Label the drawing: air and air movements, the second ingredient for weather.

Northern Hemisphere Air Movements

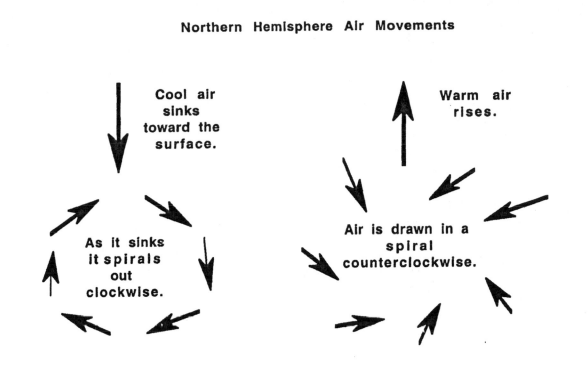

➤ Figure 9.3. Air Movements

A barometer is the instrument meteorologists use to measure air pressure. Falling air pressure indicates stormy weather, and rising air pressure promises good weather. Two instruments scientists use to measure wind are a wind vane and an anemometer. A wind vane tells the direction from which the wind is blowing; ask students to think of the meteorologist's report, describing "winds out of the northeast." A wind vane provided this information. The speed of wind is measured by an anemometer and is reported in miles or kilometers per hour; for ships and aircraft it's reported in knots per hour.

Connect

Add the wind vane (and the optional barometer and anemometer) to the weather station. Practice identifying wind directions and taking measurements from the barometer and the anemometer.

➤Activity Plan 5: Why Does It Rain?

Materials

    Glass
    Ice cubes
    Water
    Paper towel sheets, one per student
    Humidity scale (figure 9.4; enlarge it so it's easy for students to see)
    Science journals
    Weather instrument: rain gauge

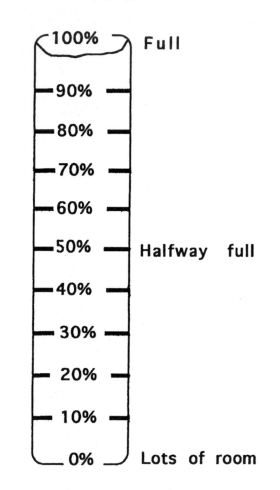

➤Figure 9.4. Humidity Scale

Engage

As you fill the glass with ice cubes and water, pose this question to students: How do we know there's water in the air? Invite speculation from the students, then observe the glass to note the moisture that has formed on the outside. When the cold glass meets the warmer surrounding air, water in the air condenses and forms droplets on the outside of the glass. Ask the students: How does it get there in the first place?

Elaborate

Wet and carefully squeeze out excess moisture in the paper towel sheets, then take them outside and place them in various locations: a shady spot, laid flat in direct sunshine, held and waved in the sunshine. Ask the students what happens to the paper towels. (The towels dry as the water evaporates.) Evaporation adds water vapor to the air. The amount of moisture (water vapor) in the air is called humidity. Show the humidity scale (see figure 9.4). When the humidity reaches the top of the scale, or 100 percent, meteorologists say the air is saturated, which means that it can't hold any more water vapor. If the humidity measures somewhere near the bottom of the scale, meteorologists say there's room for lots of water vapor in the air.

Clouds form when the air is near saturation. Have students study the sky and estimate the humidity level based on the cloud cover. (The more extensive the cloud cover, the higher the humidity.) (*Logical/Mathematical Intelligence*)

Explore

Draw figure 9.5 on the board and have students use their science journals to draw along with you. Talk about each component as you draw it.

Connect

Divide the class into five groups and have each group research and prepare posters illustrating the three basic cloud formations (cumulus, stratus, cirrus), fog, and dew. Present the posters to the class. (*Visual/Spatial and Interpersonal Intelligences*)

Set up a rain gauge in the weather station and have the students practice identifying clouds. Review the terms that will be used for reporting cloud cover on the data collection sheets: *cloudy, partly cloudy, clear.*

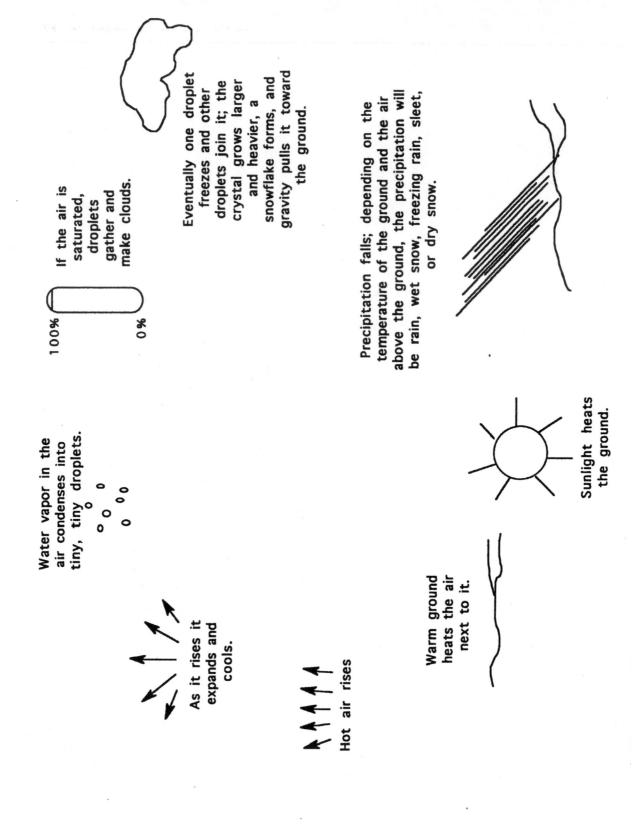

If the air is saturated, droplets gather and make clouds.

100%

0%

Eventually one droplet freezes and other droplets join it; the crystal grows larger and heavier, a snowflake forms, and gravity pulls it toward the ground.

Precipitation falls; depending on the temperature of the ground and the air above the ground, the precipitation will be rain, wet snow, freezing rain, sleet, or dry snow.

Water vapor in the air condenses into tiny, tiny droplets.

As it rises it expands and cools.

Hot air rises

Warm ground heats the air next to it.

Sunlight heats the ground.

▶ Figure 9.5. Clouds and Precipitation

➤ Activity Plan 6: The Sounds of a Rainstorm

Materials

Sandpaper blocks (Wrap sheets of sandpaper, available from hardware or lumber stores, around small wooden blocks.)
Markers and rubber bands

Engage

Have students explore soft and loud sounds in a variety of rhythm patterns:

1. Swishing hands

2. Clapping

3. Drumming on flat surfaces

4. Stomping feet

Elaborate

Tell the students: If you close your eyes and listen carefully, we can build the sounds of a rainstorm. We will have four groups and each group has an important job in creating the rainstorm:

1. Group one, you will use the sandpaper blocks. (Select group one, distribute sandpaper blocks, and have them practice their contribution.) You begin slowly and quietly swishing the blocks together, then gradually increase the movement and the noise.

2. Group two, you use the markers and the rubber bands (or your fingers), and your job is to make snapping sounds. (Select this group, distribute the supplies, and practice.) I'm counting on you being careful with the rubber bands. Here we go, let's practice. Snap the rubber band, silently count to three, and snap again; keep repeating this sound.

3. Group three, you use your hands to drum the table. (Select this group and practice.) Place your palms flat and face down on the table and begin to drum slowly and quietly, then build the speed and intensity.

4. Group four, thanks for waiting so patiently. You will stomp your feet, slowly and quietly at first but then louder and louder. (*Musical/Rhythmic Intelligence*)

Explore

Ask the students if they are ready. Tell them to watch the conductor and follow the directions. (Identify your direction signals so students know the cues; for example, finger-pointing could be the cue to begin the noise, finger to the lips could indicate a need for a quiet sound, and hands lifting with palms facing upward could signal increasing loudness and intensity.) Tell the students to begin the rainstorm.

RAINSTORM

Directions:
The sandpaper blocks slowly swish back and forth, then build in intensity.
The rubber bands and markers or fingers begin to snap (just like lightning).
Soon the hand drummers join in; the storm continues to build in intensity.
The foot stompers add their sounds, and the storm is at its height and continues
    for fifteen to twenty seconds.
Then the foot stompers begin to quiet.
The hand drummers slowly stop drumming.
The rubber bands and markers or fingers grow silent.
All that is heard are the sandpaper blocks, slowly swishing to silence.

Connect

Have the class repeat the rainstorm, then discuss what students hear and how they connect the sounds they are making to the sounds of a thunderstorm. (different intensities of rainfall created by sandpaper blocks; lightning created by markers and rubber bands or finger snapping; thunder and noise of raindrops created by drumming and stomping) Ask the students what changes they would make. Have them repeat the storm, implementing the changes.

➤Activity Plan 7: Working As Meteorologists

In working as meteorologists, students collect data about weather conditions from the weather station set up outside, and they forecast the weather for each day.

Materials

Activity sheet 9.1, Weather Station Data Collection Sheet (multiple copies)
Weather page from a newspaper
Bookmark an Internet weather site (http://www.usatoday.com/weather)

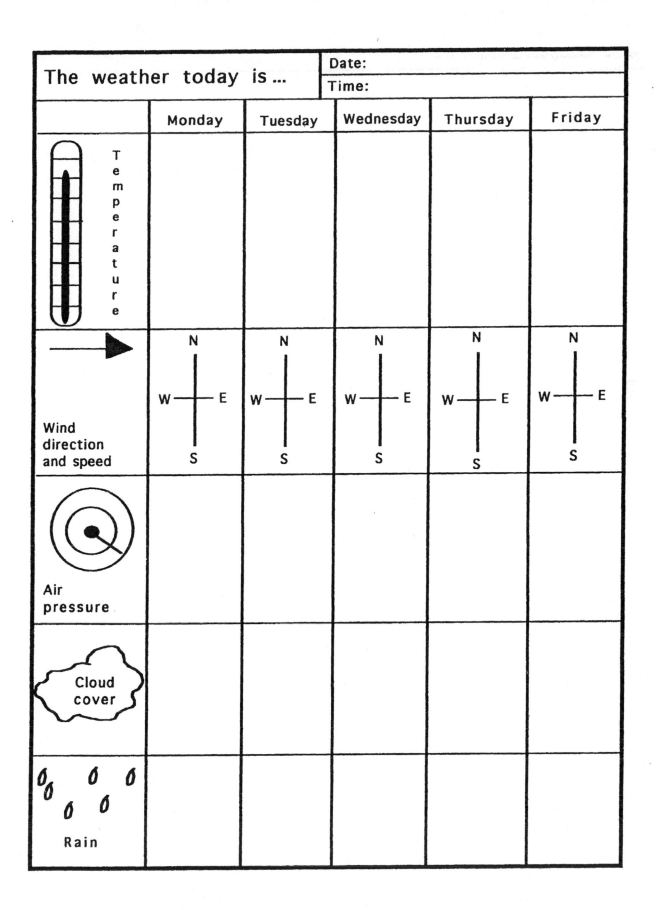

The weather today is ...	Date: Time:				
	Monday	**Tuesday**	**Wednesday**	**Thursday**	**Friday**
Temperature					
Wind direction and speed	N W—E S	N W—E S	N W—E S	N W—E S	N W—E S
Air pressure					
Cloud cover					
Rain					

➤Activity Sheet 9.1. Weather Station Data Collection Sheet

Engage

Show the newspaper weather page and brainstorm other ways to learn about the weather (radio, weather channel, Internet, other television stations). Access the Internet weather site and show students how to locate weather information for cities around the world.

Elaborate

Show students how to record weather data on the weather data collection sheets (activity sheet 9.1). Set up a schedule so students know which day will be their weather data collection and forecasting day. Students can follow the same schedule for accessing the weather site on the Internet.

Explore

Have students work with partners and prepare weather reports based on the daily data collection sheets. Encourage students to dress in costume and make the reports as entertaining as possible. Weather reports should include temperature and recommendations for dress, wind and recommendations for activities, and the type of weather (sun, rain, snow, hail, partly cloudy) and food and drink recommendations. For example, "The temperature today will be a sweltering 105 degrees with no clouds in sight. Not even a small breeze stirs the trees. Our recommendation is a hammock in the shade, tall glasses of ice-cold lemonade, lots of napping, and a good book to read. Because of the heat, wear the bare minimum; John is modeling the latest in hot-weather attire and he carries his own fan to stir the air." (*Logical/Mathematical, Interpersonal, and Bodily/Kinesthetic Intelligences*)

Connect

Have students present their weather reports to the class.

➤ Activity Plan 8: Weather—Working As Writers

In working as writers, students gather ideas (prewriting), write first drafts expressing their ideas (rough draft), conference with other student writers to review and make changes in their first drafts (revise and edit), and share their finished work (publish).

Materials

Drawing paper
Illustrating materials (watercolors, colored pencils, markers, crayons)
Activity sheet 9.2, Prewrite Pyramid (This is the brainstorming strategy for the folk story, which is one writing choice for students. Make several copies. Not every student will select this writing assignment.)
Big book story starter: "One summer on a rainy-day walk . . ." (Each student contributes a page, or students could work in partnerships and create pages.)

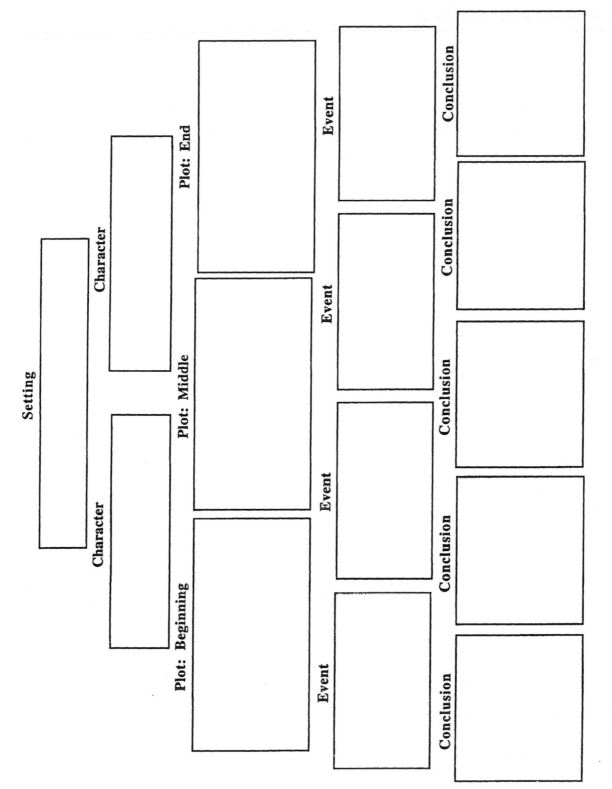

▶ Activity Sheet 9.2. Prewrite Pyramid

Engage

Tell the students that everyone will contribute a page to a big book about a rainy-day walk, but then they will have choices for their next writing assignment. Use the big book assignment to model the steps of the writing process and emphasize that each step is important and leads to wonderful, exciting, published work. For example, tell the students: We know that the theme for the big book is what might happen during a rainy-day walk. In completing the prewrite brainstorming, think of yourself, outside, on a rainy day. What are you doing? Where are you? What do you see? (As students think of ideas, record the images on the board. Ideas you might expect include puddle splashing, worms on the sidewalk, rainbows, rain on my face, dressed in a slicker, tadpoles, a sea of umbrellas, dripping tree branches, brown leaves jammed into the gutter grate, a blue jay's feather, a kite hanging by its tail.)

Elaborate

Once many ideas are listed, have students use one of the ideas from the board or another that comes to them and write pages for the story. Tell the students: Our story starter, one summer on a rainy-day walk, really allows us to write in the first person, telling what we are doing. In writing in the first person, we use words like *I, we, my, me,* and *our.* For example, if I were using the first person to write about a snowy-day experience, I would describe the experience in this way: "My feet crunched through the snow on this bright, clear, icy day; dragging my new saucer sled, I could hardly wait to reach Signet Hill and begin racing with Andrew." Write as though you are in the scene experiencing the rainy-day walk, and as you write the rough draft, don't worry about how it sounds or spelling or punctuation, just get the ideas written. (Some examples using the ideas above include: "I splashed through the puddles in my red rubber boots and watched worms crawl to safety on the sidewalk"; "I stared at the rainbow that suddenly appeared over the trees and imagined the pot of gold waiting at the end"; "I used a stick to poke and stir the brown leaves jammed into the gutter grate.")

When you have your first draft completed, read through it and begin to make changes. Meet with a peer, read it again, and make more changes. Remember that the thesaurus will help you improve your word choices. For example, after writing "I splashed through the puddles in my red rubber boots and watched worms crawl to safety on the sidewalk," you may decide to explore more interesting words for *crawl.* The thesaurus suggests *wiggle* as one choice; substitute this word so that part of the sentence now reads "watched worms wiggle to safety on the sidewalk." Or perhaps when you conferenced, your sentence didn't make sense to the person with whom you conferenced, and he/she asked several questions of explanation. How could you revise the sentence to make it clearer? In revising the first draft, your goal is to make every word show something to the reader.

Tell students that another step in changing the rough draft happens when they edit their work. Have them work with a partner to check each other's spelling, punctuation, and capitalization.

Now that the students are ready for the final copy, tell them to use the drawing paper and decide where to place the text. Point out to them that as they look at the book they can see that on most of the pages the text is placed across the bottom of the pages, some pages have the text at the top (last page and two pages near the end), and some pages have the text placed to the side or in the middle (the pages where Sylvester tests the pebble and first turns to rock). Tell them that once they have written the text using their very best handwriting, they can add an illustration to the page. (*Verbal/Linguistic and Visual/Spatial Intelligences*)

Explore

Share the writing choices and let students decide their new writing assignments. Remind them that each task card gives them the guidelines for the assignment. Circulate and conference with students as they work. (*Verbal/Linguistic Intelligence*)

Connect

Have students present their writing to the class.

RIDDLES

Write weather couplet riddles. (*Verbal/Linguistic Intelligence*)

Prewrite brainstorming
Choose a weather topic and conduct research to make a list of facts about the topic.

Rough drafting
Write the first draft of your couplet. Remember, a couplet is a two-line verse in which the end words of each line rhyme and each line contains the same number of syllables. Here's an example:

> Lightning heats the air so fast
> Then you hear my mighty blast.
> (Thunder)

Revising
Work with a partner to check the number of syllables in each line. Are they the same? Do your end words rhyme? How could you improve the words you have used?

Editing
Work with a partner to check for spelling, punctuation, and capitalization errors; make corrections.

Publishing
Type your riddle or write it using your very best handwriting.

WEATHER POEMS

Create a cinquain poem based on one of these weather words: *cloud, rain, sun, snow, tornado, hurricane, wind,* or *rainbow.* (*Verbal/Linguistic Intelligence*)

WEATHER POEMS

Prewrite Brainstorming

Fold your paper in half and fold it in half again. When you unfold the paper you have four boxes. In the first box write describing words that show what you see, in the second box write action words that describe the movements of the weather, in the third box put yourself in the scene and write how you feel, and in the fourth box think of synonyms for the weather word.

<u>Describing words</u>	<u>Action words</u>
strong gray skies windy bending trees crashing waves	raging towering blowing tearing swirling riping
<u>Feeling phrases</u> struggling against the wind hiding in the darkened house listening to the calm, waiting for the return of the storm	<u>Other words and phrases which name the subject</u> terrible storm sea storm

➤ Figure 9.6. Prewrite Brainstorming

WEATHER POEMS

Rough Drafting

Use the ideas from your prewrite brainstorming to write the first draft of your poem. Look at the poem about the cyclone (figure 9.7) and follow these rules:

Line 1: The title or subject of the poem.

Line 2: Two adjectives that describe the subject.

Line 3: Three action words that describe movements/actions of the subject.

Line 4: Short phrase expressing a feeling about the subject.

Line 5: Another name for the subject.

➤ Figure 9.7. Cyclone Poem

> Cyclone
> Fierce winds
> Blowing, tearing, swirling
> Hiding in the darkened house
> Terrible storm

WEATHER POEMS

Revising
Use the thesaurus to make your word choices more interesting; also be sure that you do not repeat words in the poem. In the cyclone poem the describing line says "fierce winds"; note that the brainstorming sheet has the word *strong*. In using the thesaurus, *fierce* was a suggested substitute for *strong* and seemed more interesting.

Editing
Work with a partner to check for spelling, punctuation, and capitalization errors; make corrections.

Publishing
Type your poem or write it using your very best handwriting.

FOLK STORIES

Working with a partner, write a weather folk story about one of these topics: How Rainbows Came to Be, Why Some Clouds Are White, How Thunder Got Its Boom, Why the Wind Blows, Why Snowflakes Have Six Sides, Why Air Is Invisible, How the Sun Came to Be So Hot, or Where Raindrops Come From. (*Verbal/Linguistic and Interpersonal Intelligences*)

Prewrite brainstorming
Use the prewrite pyramid (activity sheet 9.2) to brainstorm ideas for the story: setting, two main characters, plot summary (beginning, middle, end), events that develop the plot, and conclusions for each event and for the story.

Rough drafting
Use the ideas from your pyramid to write the first draft of your story.

Revising
One partner should read the story aloud and one partner should listen for changes that should be made. Make the suggested changes, switch roles, and read the story aloud again, then make other changes.

Editing
Work together to check for spelling, punctuation, and capitalization errors; make corrections.

Publishing
Type your story or write your story using your very best handwriting.

➤ Activity Plan 9: Weather—Working As Artists

In working as artists, students observe and imagine, sketch and plan, gather materials, and create the art piece.

Materials

Poster board; gather several sheets

Drawing paper

Activity sheet 9.3, Donkey Paper Doll (several copies; not every student will select this art choice)

Illustrating materials (crayons, colored pencils, markers)

Guinness Book of World Records (New York: Facts on File, annual)

Engage

Share the art choices and allow students to select one art activity.

Elaborate

Review the steps for working as an artist and emphasize that each step is important and leads to a wonderful art piece. For example, ask/tell the students:

1. What's the first step in creating a piece of art? (Students will probably respond with "get an idea.") Some good ways to get ideas are to observe and imagine. That's what you will be doing in these three art projects. If you are creating the reward poster, imagine how you could advertise the problem and catch people's attention. If you are creating the weather donkey doll, imagine yourself as a donkey, dressed for your favorite outdoor activity. If you are creating the weather record cartoon, use the *Guinness Book of World Records* to select a weather record, then imagine a funny scene about this record.

2. Once you have an idea, plan how it will look and then sketch it.

3. The third step is gathering supplies. What will you need to create the art project?

4. Now you are ready to create your art piece. Look at your sketch and begin to create!

Explore

Have students begin working on their art choices. Display the steps to guide students as they work. Circulate and conference with students.

Connect

Display the artwork and tour the display, inviting each student to share as you reach his or her art piece.

➤Activity Sheet 9.3. Donkey Paper Doll

REWARD POSTERS

Sylvester was lost to his family and friends for a whole year. Work with a partner to create missing posters advertising for the lost Sylvester. One of you will be the writer and one of you will be the artist; you will both share in the presentation. Be really dramatic when you share the poster. (*Interpersonal and Visual/Spatial Intelligences*)

WEATHER PEOPLE

Dress the donkey paper doll (activity sheet 9.3) for its favorite outdoor activity.

Look at the examples (figure 9.8) and create a card that describes the outfit and the outdoor activity. (*Visual/Spatial and Verbal/Linguistic Intelligences*)

Susie is dressed for a spring trip to the zoo. She is carrying her umbrella in case it rains, and she has tucked her rubber boots into her backpack.

Sylvester is perfectly dressed for a skiing trip. Notice his layers of clothing: a bright red cotton turtleneck, a blue-and-white striped sweater, and his purple down-filled parka. He sports a pair of the latest style in goggles.

➤ Figure 9.8. Weather Descriptions

WEATHER RECORDS

Use the *Guinness Book of World Records* to choose a weather record. Create a cartoon picture that gives information about the record. For example, a cartoon for most rainy days could show a person looking drenched and huddling under an umbrella on Mt. Waialeale on Kuaui in Hawaii, and the conversation bubble could say, "No sun again!! This sure is a rainy year—350 days of rain." (*Visual/Spatial and Verbal/Linguistic Intelligences*)

➤ Culminating Activity Plan

Materials

Sandwich supplies (wheat or oat bread, cheese spread, sprouts)
Oatmeal cookies
Herb tea
Invitations to parents

Celebrate the book unit with a spring picnic. Serve the sandwiches, cookies, and herbal tea—all foods enjoyed by Sylvester and his family. Display students' work and have students select and share favorite pieces (one favorite per student).

10 A Tree Is Nice

Written by Janice May Udry
Illustrated by Marc Simont
New York: Harper & Row, 1956

Summary

➤ Pictures and words share the importance for our world of trees, which provide beauty and shade, lots of opportunities for play, a safe haven for all kinds of animals, and fruit and nuts. It's also fun to watch one grow.

Award Year

➤ 1957

Art Information

➤ Illustrated using gouache over watercolor.

Curriculum Connections

➤ Trees, with emphasis on this science idea: Trees are a valuable resource; they change with the seasons and because of their cycle of growth.

➤ Activity Plan 1: Sharing the Story

Materials

> Caldecott Award poster
> Gouache pigment (available at art stores)
> Watercolor paints (available at art stores)
> Paintbrush
> Small cup of water
> Open bulletin board space (for the "trees are important" collage)
> Drawing paper
> Illustrating materials (crayons, markers, colored pencils)

Engage

Have students dramatize the growth of a mighty oak tree as follows (*Bodily/Kinesthetic Intelligence*):

- You are an acorn waiting to grow because a squirrel has just buried you in the ground. (Students should crouch and curl into a tight ball.)

- The soil has warmed and water flows by you; springtime is here at last. (Students should uncurl a little.)

- Slowly you grow a root or two and then a sprout pushes up through the soil to the sun above. (Students should spread their feet as though they are roots digging deep into the soil and slowly extend a hand as though a sprout is pushing through the soil.)

- Warm summer rains fill the ground; your trunk becomes sturdy and soon sprouts another branch. (Students should slowly rise from the crouching position until they are standing straight, then slowly extend the other hand and arm as though the tree is branching.)

- Your roots dig deeper and your branches spread out; year after year you continue to grow. (Students should spread their feet a little more and extend their arms and bodies until they are standing on tiptoes.)

- Winds blow, softly, gently, then a furious storm whips your branches and dies away. Sunshine returns and children play under your shady umbrella. (Students should sway gently, then furiously, then gently again, then stand still and arc their hands to provide shade for the children at play.)

- Fall comes, acorns fall again; your leaves sift to the ground; it's winter again. (Students should pretend to drop acorns from their hands, rustle their hands as though leaves are falling, then stand still for winter.)

Elaborate

Have students share favorite tree experiences.

Explore

Tell students: You have shared your favorite tree experiences, now let's see why Ms. Udry thinks trees are nice.

Connect

Share the Caldecott Award information:

1. As students examine the cover of the book, ask them what special thing they notice. (gold medal) Ask them what the name of the medal is. (Caldecott Award Medal) Ask them why it has been placed on this book. (Some answers might be: The illustrations are special, well done, particularly interesting, exciting, and/or unusual.)

2. Discuss the art techniques used in creating the pictures. Full-color pictures alternate with black-and-white illustrations. The gouache (opaque watercolor) painted over the watercolor adds vibrancy to the full-color illustrations. Point out the brightness of the leaves and the sky in the fall picture, the apples and clothing of the children on the apple tree page, and the snow and house in the wind-blown winter illustration. (Re-create the effect by painting some shape with the watercolor, then painting over it with the gouache pigment.)

3. Ask two student volunteers to search the poster for the year the story won. (Searching the poster helps students become familiar with the many different titles selected for the award.)

Discuss the ideas from the story. What are other ways that trees are useful and important for the world? Some responses might be: oxygen for the world (humans, animals, insects, fish, reptiles), fruits, silk (silkworms eat mulberry leaves), houses, paper, fences, garages, office buildings, rubber, turpentine, cork (bottle stoppers, bulletin boards, floats for fishing, floor coverings), fuel, and medicines. Have students create a bulletin board collage that illustrates the importance of trees. Encourage them to use as many real objects as they can in making the collage. (*Verbal/Linguistic and Visual/Spatial Intelligences*)

➤ Activity Plan 2: Interdependence— The World of a Tree

Materials

Rulers, one per student partnership
Small circle, two to three inches in diameter, made from construction paper
Science journals
String for measuring the trunk of the tree
Outdoor setting planning (Select a tree for observation; in selecting the tree choose one that shows the diversity of life supported by the tree: birds, squirrels, insects, and plants.)

Engage

Sketch a tree on the board and write these measurements: 367 feet tall, 10 feet in diameter. According to the 1998 *Guinness Book of World Records*, these are the measurements of the tallest tree, a redwood in Ukiah, California. Scientists estimate that the tree is 1,000 years old.

Elaborate

Have students use rulers to measure and see the dimensions of this tree:

1. Represent the diameter of the tree: In an open space in the classroom, place a small circle on the floor and have students measure five feet from that center point, then stand in a circle, facing the center, arms extended. (See figure 10.1.)

2. Represent the height of the tree: Have students think about a football field from goal post to goal post, because this distance equals 360 feet, and the world-record tree is just 7 feet longer than this distance. Walk the hallways of the school or the grounds outdoors to measure the height of the tree.

Tell the students: If the tree is 1,000 years old, imagine the birds, animals, and insects who have used its branches and the ground underneath. Let's explore an outdoor setting to observe the world of a tree. (Remind students to bring their science journals, pencils, and the rulers.) (*Logical/ Mathematical and Bodily/Kinesthetic Intelligences*)

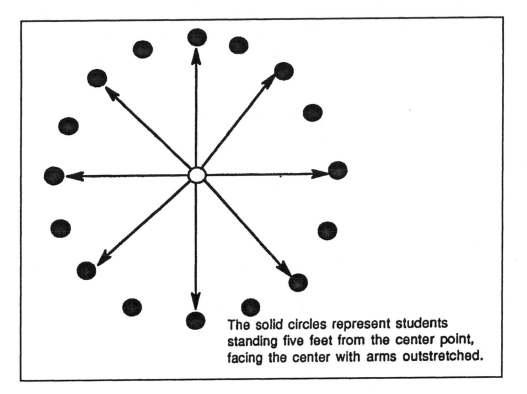

The solid circles represent students standing five feet from the center point, facing the center with arms outstretched.

➤Figure 10.1. Measuring the Diameter of the Tree

Explore

Have students complete the following observations and activities. (*Naturalist, Logical/ Mathematical, and Bodily/Kinesthetic Intelligences*)

- Observation 1: Sit and observe the tree, then draw the tree.

- Observation 2: Use the string to measure the circumference of the tree; measure about three feet from the base of the tree. Lay the string on the ground and use the rulers to identify the measurement. Record the measurement in your science journals. How does this measurement compare with the world-record tree?

- Observation 3: Estimate the height of the tree. I would like one of you to stand ten to fifteen steps from the tree and extend your arm in front of you, holding a pencil. Line up the bottom of the pencil with the base of the tree and slowly walk backward until the tip of the pencil lines up with the top of the tree. (See figure 10.2.) Mark this spot (if the tree fell, the top of the tree would reach this spot). Now measure the distance from the tree to your stopping point. Record this measurement in your science journals. How does this measurement compare with the height of the world-record tree?

- Observation 4: Illustrate the life around and in the tree:

   1. What plants and flowers live under the tree?
   2. Can fungi, algae, and lichens be found? (Look at the ground around the tree and on the trunk of the tree.)
   3. What parasites do you see? (mistletoe, ivy, other vines)
   4. What animals do you see?
   5. What insects do you see?
   6. If dead leaves are collected under the tree, turn and lift some of them. What do you observe?

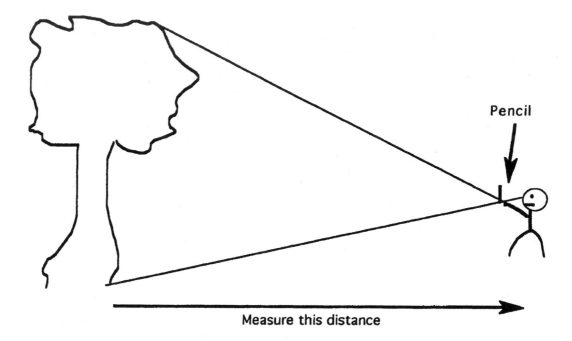

➤Figure 10.2. Estimating the Height of the Tree

Connect

Have students reflect on the meaning of interdependence. Ask them to explain how the tree is an example of this concept. (The animals need the tree for food and shelter, insects and bacteria break down the dead leaves to provide rich soil full of nutrients for the tree and the plants and flowers that grow at its base.) (*Visual/Spatial and Intrapersonal Intelligences*)

➤ Activity Plan 3: Structures— Looking at Seeds and Sorting

Materials

Science journals

Assortment of seeds, one container per student partnership; include fruit seeds (oranges, apples, peaches, pears, cherries, etc.), nuts (walnut, pecan, almond, etc.), acorns (oak), seeds with wings (linden and maple), pods (catalpa, locust, redbud), pinecones (larch, pine, spruce), and catkins (birch, willow, aspen, cottonwood)

Graph paper or a graphing software program

Engage

Hold up some seeds in front of the class and say: "A seed is a tree just waiting to grow. As you can see there are many kinds of seeds."

Elaborate

Ask the students: What do you suppose would grow from this one? Why? And this one? Why? (Continue with several examples until students lose interest.)

Explore

Display a container of seeds and ask students what criteria they might use to sort the seeds. (Students' responses will vary, but may include: color, shape, size, texture, edible/inedible, source, e.g., fruit trees, nut trees, evergreen trees, etc.) Have students work with partners, examine seeds thoroughly, and choose two different ways to sort them. After the first sorting, have students record this information in their science journals:

The first time we sorted the seeds we grouped them by _____ (for example, color)

This means that _____ (For example, we chose light and dark as our color requirements and sorted the seeds into two piles, then we organized them in a row from lightest to darkest in color.)

Here are our results (draw the results):

Have students sort the containers a second time and record the following information in their science journals:

The second time we sorted the seeds we grouped them by _____ (for example, texture)

This means that _____ (For example, we chose rough and smooth and sorted them into two piles.)

Here are our results (draw the results):

Connect

Begin a class discussion and ask students to share how they sorted the seeds. How many used size? color? texture? shape? source? edible/inedible? other? (Record the responses on the board.) Ask the students what criteria they used for sorting.

- size (For example, were the seeds sorted into small, medium, and large piles, or in a row from smallest to largest, or seeds smaller than an inch and seeds larger than an inch, or using other factors?)

- color (Light and dark seeds, white, brown, and black seeds, or other factors?)

- texture (Smooth and rough, soft and hard, prickly and smooth?)

- shape (Long and short, winged and round, narrow and wide, fat and thin?)

- source (Fruit trees, nut trees, evergreens, deciduous?)

Record on the board the organizing information students used and save it for the creative writing assignment that follows the sorting exercise. Use graph paper or a computer graphing program to graph the seed-sorting results. Which way of sorting was most popular? Why? Which way of sorting was least popular? Why? Which way of sorting was most unusual? Why? (*Logical/Mathematical and Interpersonal Intelligences*)

Conclude the sorting exercise with a creative writing assignment in which students choose the kinds of seed they wish to be, then describe what would happen to them. Have students use the words that have been listed on the board as choices for the first part of their writing assignment. They may choose more than one idea. For example, "If I were a seed I would choose to be small and round and smooth. Then I could . . ." Ask the students: What could you do or where could you go or what might you see or what experience might you have if you were small and round and smooth? (Require students to choose words and ideas that were not used in the class example; for example, maybe they choose to be a winged seed that floats and soars in the wind or maybe they choose to be a prickly seed that loves to attach itself to a wandering sock.) (*Verbal/Linguistic Intelligence*)

➤ Activity Plan 4: Structures—What's in a Seed?

Materials

Science journals
Variety of seeds that are easy to dissect (lima, pinto, kidney)
Rulers
Small cups
Water
Paper towels
Permanent markers
Magnifying glasses

Engage

Address the students as follows: We have been looking at different kinds of seeds, but now we want to determine how seeds are alike. What do you think? How are all seeds alike? (Students may give you this information, but may not until after the investigation: Each seed contains a tiny plant, stored food, and an outer skin. Accept and speculate based on the responses you do get.)

Elaborate

Tell the students: In talking about how seeds are alike, there are some new vocabulary words we want to be sure to know. (Write the following words and definitions on the board and have students record them in their science journals.)

- *Embryo*: This is the tiny plant inside the seed. It is waiting to grow.

- *Stored food*: This is food inside the seed that the embryo uses to grow.

- *Seed coat*: This is the outer skin of the seed. It protects the other parts of the seed from injury, insects, and loss of water.

Explore

Tell the students that you will now compare seeds to see if they are alike based on the criteria students identified in the "Engage" step of the lesson. Ask them if they can explain what you are hoping to prove or find out by conducting this experiment. Discuss this with the class and have them agree on an outcome for the experiment. For example: "We will examine several kinds of seeds to prove that all seeds are alike in three ways: They have a seed coat and they contain stored food and an embryo. This is how scientists work. They raise questions like our question: How are seeds alike? Then, based on their research and knowledge they think about what the answer should be or what they hope to prove. We hope to prove that seeds are alike in three ways: They have a seed coat and they contain stored food and an embryo. This is the hypothesis for the experiment. Use your science journals to record the hypothesis for the experiment." Be sure to use the language students have given as you review and confirm the hypothesis.

Have students write the names of their seeds in their journals and spend some time examining the seeds, then write short descriptions of how they look and feel. Draw and color pictures of the seeds. Measure the seeds: lengths, widths, and thicknesses. (*Visual/Spatial Intelligence*)

Have students write their names on paper cups, then bring their cups and their beans to a central spot in the classroom. Help them fill their cups with water and allow the beans to soak overnight. Complete the experiment on the second day. (See Activity Plan 5. The "Connect" exercise is also in that plan.) (*Logical/Mathematical Intelligence*)

➤ Activity Plan 5: What's in a Seed? Part Two

Materials

Science journals
Rulers
Soaked seeds
Magnifying glasses

Engage

Have students review the hypothesis: For example, "Seeds are alike in three ways: They have a seed coat and they contain stored food and an embryo." Be sure to use the language that the students have used.

Elaborate

Have students continue the process of examining their seeds. They should carefully examine the soaked seeds and then write short descriptions of how they look and feel now that they have soaked in water overnight. Have them draw and color pictures of the seeds; carefully measure the seeds; and record the lengths, the widths, and the thicknesses. (Have students carefully handle the seeds so they don't remove the seed coats during this step.) (*Visual/Spatial Intelligence*)

Ask the students how the seeds changed after they were soaked. (Let students record their ideas in their science journals before beginning a class discussion about this. Then record their responses on the board. Look at the responses and make generalizations about the relationship between water and seed growth.) Based on the class discussion, have students use their science journals to summarize in their own words why water is important for seed growth. (Water softens the seed coat and moves through it, then the seed coat splits and the embryo starts to grow.)

Explore

Have students continue to investigate by finding the beans' outside skins or coverings and carefully slipping these coats off the seed. Have students describe how they feel and look, then record in their journals what the seed looks like after the coats have been removed.

Tell the students to carefully open the seeds and find the embryos, then make drawings of what they see. They can use magnifying glasses to observe the embryos more closely. Ask them how many leaves the seeds have.

Discuss with the class the location of the embryos. Ask them: Where in the seeds were the embryos? How do the sizes of the embryos compare with the stored food parts? Why is this?

Connect

Discuss the experiment and draw conclusions: "Our hypothesis was that all seeds are alike in three ways: They would contain an embryo and stored food and they would be protected by a seed coat. Is this proven? Why?" Based on the class discussion, have students use their science journals to summarize in their own words the results of the experiment.

Review the experiment to list the safety precautions students followed and have students record the safety precautions in their journals. (careful handling of the seeds, care with the magnifying glasses, respect for the seeds and materials of others) (*Logical/Mathematical Intelligence*)

➤ Activity Plan 6: Adaptations—How Seeds Travel

Materials

Apple
Bean, pumpkin, corn, and pea seeds
Tape
Construction paper
Paste
Materials to use for adaptations: rubber bands, toothpicks, balloons, scissors, pencils, plastic bags, cork, cotton, feathers, tacks, metal springs, wire

Engage

Cut open the apple and extract and count the number of seeds inside. Ask the students: How many seeds are in one apple? How many apple trees could grow from the seeds? Why don't apple trees cover the earth? Why do seeds have dispersal mechanisms? Refocus question: What might happen if maple seeds fell straight to the ground and grew right under the mother maple? (not enough light or room to grow, fewer nutrients)

Elaborate

Ask the students: What are other seed dispersal mechanisms? Refocus question: What are ways seeds travel? Brainstorm some ideas and locate a source to share about how seeds travel. (A dandelion puff is light enough to be blown by the wind, other seeds are sticky or prickly and stick to surfaces, other seeds are round and roll.)

Explore

Have students work with partners to experiment with seed dispersal. Have each partnership choose one of these dispersal problems and invent a solution to the problem. They should then demonstrate and explain the dispersal invention. (*Interpersonal and Bodily/Kinesthetic Intelligences*)

- Adapt a seed so it will float on water at least five minutes.
- Adapt a seed so it will be thrown at least two feet away from the parent plant.
- Adapt a seed so it will attract a bird or an animal.
- Adapt a seed so it will hitchhike on an animal or person for twenty feet.
- Adapt a seed so it will fly for at least three feet.

Connect

Take a walk with the students in an outdoor setting. Be sure to step in damp areas and walk through high grass to pick up seeds on the soles of the shoes and have things attach to socks. Scrape the shoes and shake the socks over a tray of potting soil when students return. See if anything grows.

➤Activity Plan 7: Structures—The Parts of the Tree

Materials

Science journals
Outdoor setting (Choose a setting with lots of different trees because students will be making bark rubbings.)
Drawing paper
String

Crayons
Variety of leaves (broad leaves like oak, maple, and birch, and spiky leaves like cedar, pine, and spruce)

Engage

Have students fold pages in their journals into thirds and draw the three main parts of the tree: roots, trunk, and crown. At the bottom fold they should draw a wavy line (the ground) and draw a tap root and branching root system through the bottom third of the page. They should use the middle section to draw the trunk of the tree and use the top third to draw the crown, leaves, branches, and twigs. (See figure 10.3.) (*Visual/Spatial Intelligence*)

Elaborate

As you conduct the discussion, have students record summary information in their journals. Ask them: What is the job of the roots? (collect water and minerals, take in oxygen) What is the job of the trunk? (carry sugar from the leaves and branches to the rest of the tree, carry water and minerals from the soil to the branches and leaves, support the branches and leaves) What protects the trunk? (bark) What is the job of the bark? (protects against heat and cold, prevents the tree from drying out, keeps insects and bacteria out)

Have students walk to the outdoor setting (with their journals) and work with partners to take bark rubbings from a variety of trees. To take a rubbing, they need to position the paper on the trunk, tie the paper to the tree with the string, and rub the paper with the crayon. Students will probably want to make several rubbings, so have plenty of paper and string. When students have taken several rubbings, gather together and continue the discussion about bark. Ask them what observations they can make about the barks. (Some bark is smooth, some is really wrinkled and rough.) Ask them: If the bark works like a skin, why isn't it smooth? (It isn't stretchy like our skin but cracks when the tree grows; however, if the tree is healthy, the cracks aren't deep enough to break completely through the bark.) Have students record this information in their science journals. (*Bodily/Kinesthetic and Visual/ Spatial Intelligences*)

Explore

Return to the classroom and let students examine a variety of deciduous and evergreen leaves to discover the differences, noticing shapes, vein structures, and outer surfaces. (*Visual/Spatial Intelligence*)

Connect

Ask the students: What is the job of the leaves? (help in the process of making food for the tree) Why do some trees lose their leaves in fall? (Trees cannot take in water through their roots in cold, wintry weather. This means they would dehydrate, or dry up, if they didn't drop their leaves before winter. Dropping leaves in fall helps them conserve moisture.) What protects evergreen trees from dehydration? (These leaves have a hard, waxy layer as a covering; they also have a smaller surface area from which to lose water.) Have students record this information in their science journals.

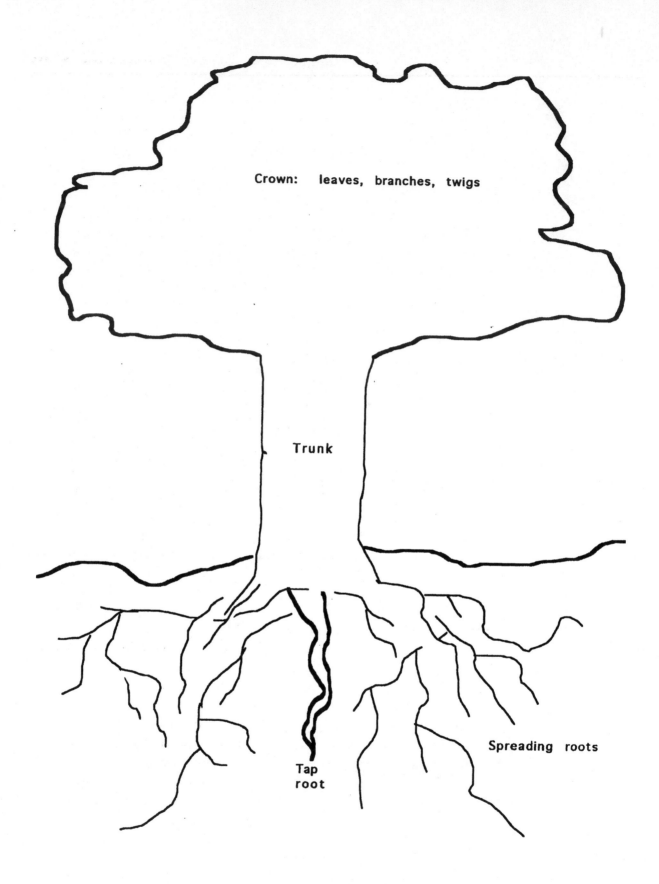

Crown: leaves, branches, twigs

Trunk

Spreading roots

Tap root

➤Figure 10.3. Parts of the Tree

➤Activity Plan 8: Structures—Stems

Materials

Straws and cups of water, one per student
Musical instruments (harmonica, flute, slide whistle, recorder—anything that can be an image of a conduit)
Mason jar
Water
Two baggies
Two rubber bands
Science journals

Engage

Introduce the idea of a conduit, something that helps something move from one place to another. Use your musical instruments as examples. Have students sip water, swallow it, then blow through the straw to release carbon dioxide into the air. Suggest the idea of railroad tracks. Ask them how the tracks represent a conduit. (*Musical/Rhythmic and Bodily/Kinesthetic Intelligences*)

Elaborate

Have students work in partnerships to brainstorm and share other examples of conduits. (*Interpersonal Intelligence*)

Explore

Take a walk in the outdoor setting with the students to look at a variety of plants (shrubs, trees, plants, grasses); have students think about this question as they explore: How is the stem/trunk a conduit? (transports sugar, water, and minerals through the tree)

Gather two freshly cut stems (one should have leaves and one should have the leaves removed). Have students set up an experiment to observe and compare the transport action of the stems. They should fill half the jar with water and add the stems. On the stem with leaves, they will enclose some of the leaves in a baggy and close the baggy with a rubber band; on the stem without leaves, they will enclose the end of a branch in a baggy and close the baggy with a rubber band. Have students predict what will happen if they leave the stems in water overnight. Have them make drawings of the setup and record their predictions in their science journals. Leave the jars overnight.

Connect

The next day, have the students examine the stems and discuss what has happened. Ask them: How does what happened compare with their predictions? How is the stem a conduit? Why is this important for the survival of the plant? Have students record their reflections in their science journals. (*Logical/Mathematical and Intrapersonal Intelligences*)

➤ Activity Plan 9: Structures—Leaves

Materials

Variety of leaves, one per student partnership

Green crayons or pencils

Photosynthesis skit from *The Growing Classroom: Garden-Based Science* by Roberta Jaffe and Gary Appel, 1990, page 142. (Available from Scott Foresman-Addison-Wesley Publishing Company, Menlo Park, CA, 800-552-2259; ISBN: 0-201-21539-X.)

Engage

Write this statement on the board: "Leaves are the energy factories of trees." Pose these questions: What do you do when you are hungry? What do animals do? How do trees get food? Leaves play an important role in making food, and that's why we consider leaves the energy factories of trees. What are three ingredients plants need to make food? (water, light, air, carbon dioxide)

Elaborate

Have students work with partners to examine leaves up close. Have them use their science journals to draw the shapes of their leaves. Tell them to look closely at the vein structure and add this structure to the drawings. Ask them what the job of the veins of the leaves is. (carry water, nutrients, gases, and other materials to and from all parts of a leaf; provide support and help position the leaves to get sunlight)

The outer surface of most leaves contains many small pores. Have students add tiny dots to their drawings and label them. Tell them to think about the function of pores in humans and explain what they think the job of pores in leaves is. (allow carbon dioxide to come in and oxygen to be released, release excess water)

Leaves are filled with hundreds of cells and inside these cells are small structures called chloroplasts. Have students draw small circles in the leaves, then label the circles. Chloroplasts contain a special green pigment called chlorophyll; without this chlorophyll light energy could not be trapped. Have students add green to the circles. (*Visual/Spatial and Interpersonal Intelligences*)

Explore

Dramatize the photosynthesis skit from *The Growing Classroom*. (*Bodily/Kinesthetic Intelligence*)

Connect

Based on the dramatization, have students reflect on this question in their journals: How are leaves the energy factories of plants? (*Intrapersonal Intelligence*)

➤ Activity Plan 10: Life Cycles

Materials

Science journals
Illustrating materials (crayons, markers, colored pencils)

Engage

Have students use their bodies to demonstrate knowledge and understanding of a tree from seed to an adult (seed, seedling, sapling, tree). (*Bodily/Kinesthetic Intelligence*)

Elaborate

Identify and list the stages in the life cycle of trees.

Explore

Have students draw the life cycle of trees. (*Visual/Spatial Intelligence*)

Connect

Share and discuss the drawings.

➤ Activity Plan 11: Life Cycles—Decomposers

Materials

Decomposers bag (One week before starting the activity, place pieces of old fruit, cheese, and moist bread in a clear gallon plastic bag. Hang the bag on a bulletin board with a sign reading, "What do you think is happening in this bag?")
Bag of leaves
Outdoor setting planning: find evidence of decomposition (rotting log, forest floor)
Science journals

Engage

Dump the bag of leaves and ask students what happens to the leaves that trees drop each season (besides raking and being taken to the landfill). Ask them why we aren't buried in leaves.

Elaborate

Focus students' attention on the materials in the plastic bag that is hanging up. Ask them what changes they notice and what they think is happening to the ingredients. Ask them why this process is important for the world and where they have seen examples of once-living things changing and decomposing in the environment. (rotting log, compost piles, forest floor, moldy garbage)

Explore

Explore the outdoor setting for rotting logs or other evidence of decomposition. Turn over the log and note all the insects that scurry away. Have students record examples in their science journals. (*Visual/Spatial Intelligence*)

Connect

Tell students that they have seen the beginning of the way in which an important part of the soil is made. The part that comes from dead plants and animals is called organic matter. Ask them: What does organic matter add to the soil? Why is it valuable? How is decomposition part of the life cycle of a tree? Have students reflect in their journals about the role of decomposition in nature. (*Intrapersonal Intelligence*)

➤ Activity Plan 12: Seasonal Fun—The Seasons of a Tree

Materials

Drawing paper
Illustrating materials (crayons, markers, colored pencils, watercolors)

Engage

Have students fold drawing paper sheets in half, then in half again, so they have four columns.

Elaborate

Explain to students that they will use the four columns to illustrate the seasons of a tree. For example, if students choose to illustrate an apple tree, the spring picture would show an apple tree covered in blossoms, the summer drawing would show green leaves and small apples not yet ripe, the fall picture would depict ripe apples and leaves beginning to turn, the winter scene would show bare branches. If students choose to show the seasons of an evergreen tree, change would be more evident in the setting of the tree than in the tree itself.

Explore

Have students create their seasons of a tree drawings. (*Visual/Spatial and Logical/Mathematical Intelligences*)

Connect

Have students share their pictures. Invite discussion about similarities among the trees throughout the seasons.

➤ Culminating Activity Plan: Plant a Tree

Have students work in small groups to identify places on the school grounds where they might plant trees. Ask them to find out what kind of trees would work best and what watering and soil needs the trees have. (*Verbal/Linguistic, Bodily/Kinesthetic, and Interpersonal Intelligences*)

11 The Caldecott Award

➤ Activity Plan: A Look at Randolph Caldecott

Materials

Selection of Caldecott Award books that show the gold medal

Audiovisual resource on Randolph Caldecott (*Randolph Caldecott: The Man Behind the Medal* is one suggestion. It's a video from Weston Woods, 12 Oakwood Ave., Norwalk, CT 06850, 800-243-5020; cost: $39.00.)

Picture books illustrated by Randolph Caldecott

Various resources giving information about Randolph Caldecott (Most encyclopedias have information, and you can use the Internet to access the Randolph Caldecott home page at http://www.ala.org/alsc/caldecott.html.)

Preplanning with the librarian (In addition to the book chosen as the Caldecott Award winner each year, honor books are also named. Gather a selection of honor books so that each student in the class will have one for independent reading; a list of honor books is available through this Internet site: http://www.ala.org/alsc/caldecott.html.)

Chart paper

Drawing paper

Illustrating materials (crayons, colored pencils, markers)

Transparency of figure 11.1

Cinquain Poem Form

Name
Two describing words (adjectives)
Three action words (verbs)
Four-word phrase giving new information about the person
One- or two-word synonym for the person

Eric Carle
Bold, brilliant
Imagined, wrote, illustrated
A Very Hungry Caterpillar
Author

Stair Poem Form

One- or two-word synonym for the person

Four-word phrase telling the location of the person

Three describing words

Name of the person

Great inventor
Experimenting in his laboratory
Imaginative, creative genius
Thomas Edison

➤ Figure 11.1. Rules for Writing Cinquain and Stair Poems

Engage

Display the Caldecott Award books and point to the gold medals. Ask students what criteria they would use to determine gold medal books. (Create a web listing their answers; see figure 11.2 for some anticipated responses.)

The Caldecott Award program began in 1938, and it was named in honor of Randolph Caldecott, a nineteenth-century illustrator of children's books and stories.

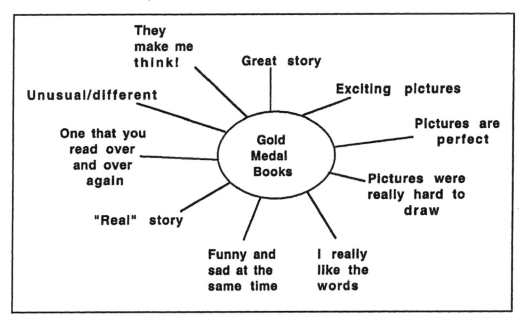

➤ Figure 11.2. Criteria for Choosing Gold Medal Books

Elaborate

Show the class the Caldecott program. Set a purpose for viewing: As you watch and listen, why do you think the library association named the award in honor of Caldecott? Refocus question: How was his style of illustrating "gold medal" quality? (Lifelike characters and scenes filled with humor, imagination, and action seem to be characteristics of his illustrations.)

Have students work with partners to gather more information about Caldecott. (In preparation for this research, bookmark the Internet site cited in the materials list; encourage some partnerships to begin with the encyclopedias while other partnerships use the Internet site. Circulate and flip-flop sources when you see students may need second sources.)

Explore

Use figure 11.1 to model and give directions on writing cinquain or stair poems. Have students use their research information and write cinquain or stair poems about the life and work of Randolph Caldecott. Post a portrait of Caldecott (available from the Web site listed above) in the center of the bulletin board. Have students present their poems to the class. Then display the poems around the portrait. (*Verbal/Linguistic and Interpersonal Intelligences*)

Connect

Travel to the library to select Caldecott honor books for independent reading. After students read the books, have them draw pictures of favorite scenes from the books and label the pictures with titles and authors. Before adding the pictures to the bulletin board display, have students present their pictures to the class, give brief summaries of the stories, and explain why they think the books were chosen as award-winning honor books. (*Verbal/Linguistic and Visual/Spatial Intelligences*)

Glossary

Acrylics: pigments that dry quickly; can be used thick or thinned with water

Casein: pigments made from milk curds

Charcoal: soft, burnt-wood sticks or pencils

Collage: materials and objects pasted over a surface

Colored pencils: colored graphite pencils

Gesso: white pigment mixed with whiting, water, and glue; used to size (prepare) canvases

Glaze: a layer of transparent color applied over the body color

Gouache: pigments mixed with white chalk and water that become opaque when applied

Graphite: soft carbon, used in pencils instead of lead

Gums: binding mediums

India ink: drawing ink made from gas black and adhesive

Inks: transparent dyes

Line drawings: pictures drawn using lines, usually not including tone or shading

Lithographic pencil: compound of grease, wax, and lampblack

Oil pastels: pigments mixed with chalk, oil, and gum and dried and formed into crayons

Oils: pigments used with turpentine or linseed oil; may be opaque or transparent

Pastel paper: textured paper

Pastels: pigments mixed with chalk, water, and gum and dried and formed into crayons

Pen and ink: drawings made using dip pens and a variety of inks

Pigments: powdered colors made from natural (rocks, earth, plants, fruit, insects, and shellfish) and chemical substances

Tempera: pigments emulsified with oil and egg

Wash: highly diluted and thinned application of color

Watercolors: very finely ground pigments that are combined with gum and mixed with water

Whiting: very finely ground powdered chalk

Woodcuts: designs cut into well-seasoned, dried wood

Index

About the Author

Shan Glandon works in the Jenks Public Schools as a library media specialist and teaches summer courses at Tulsa Community College. She is active in the Oklahoma Library Association and conducts workshops and presentations on implementing flexible scheduling and connecting the library to the classroom. In her spare time she loves to read, bike ride, and enjoy the arts (plays, concerts, museums, and art galleries).